Praise for *We Go On*

"Readers can tell when authors write with ink they've never gotten on their hands, speaking to things they know nothing about. The words on these pages haven't been written theoretically from some insulated cubicle safe from life's harms. John Onwuchekwa teaches us how to connect wisdom from the sacred pages of Scripture to the blistering pavement of our flesh-and-blood realities. He also teaches us how to keep our heads on straight when we're applauded for worldly successes as well as how to live our lives getting back up when we're down for the count and helping others up. *We Go On* reaches straight into the soul of the reader where our deepest fears and darkest doubts and fiercest anxieties reside, injecting solid, timeless truth. And where there is truth, there is hope."

—BETH MOORE, LIVING PROOF MINISTRIES

"In *We Go On*, John Onwuchekwa . . . allows us to see what many men of God don't: his struggles, his issues, his doubts. In a word, his humanity. But praise God that Onwuchekwa doesn't stop at admitting that he experiences the same challenges as the rest of us. He also shows us the way to overcome and to triumph."

—CHRIS BROUSSARD, SPORTS BROADCASTER AND NBA ANALYST, FOUNDER AND PRESIDENT OF THE K.I.N.G. MOVEMENT

"I could not put this book down. These words speak hope to despair, understanding to confusion, empathy to suffering, purpose to aimlessness, and life to death. John has masterfully brought the wisdom of the book of Ecclesiastes into our own stories, and into the reality of the world in which we live."

—CHRISTINE CAINE, FOUNDER A21 AND PROPEL WOMEN

"John and I have bonded over many things throughout the years. One . . . of the deepest connections we have has been around the book of Ecclesiastes. . . . *We Go On* pulls from the wisdom teachings of Solomon and infuses it with his unique experience and perspective. John is a dynamic thinker and communicator. His voice is so needed in a time like this."

—ANDY MINEO, AWARD-WINNING HIP HOP ARTIST

"Solomon's ancient wisdom comes to us by way of John's clear and contemporary articulation of it. With the lightheartedness of a friend and the pastoral burden of a shepherd, John explores themes we either know well or will know soon. His words will surely help us embrace the ride that is life. Buckle up."

—JACKIE HILL PERRY, BESTSELLING AUTHOR AND SPEAKER

"With refreshing honesty, relatable stories, and encouraging truth, John Onwuchekwa captures the hearts and minds of readers with this incredible journey through the book of Ecclesiastes. . . .My soul feels rested after reading through these pages!"

—DANIELLE COKE, ILLUSTRATOR AND ADVOCATE

"*We Go On* is full of truth, beautifully written, and endlessly practical. You feel like you're sitting down for coffee with a wise friend and having a brutally honest conversation about life. . . . *We Go On* is cold water for a thirsty generation, and I promise you won't regret reading it."

—TRIP LEE, AWARD-WINNING HIP HOP ARTIST AND AUTHOR

"John shows us throughout this book with his own personal stories of tragedy and triumph how we as followers of Jesus can experience both sorrow and joy simultaneously. God's word is the ultimate solid rock for all of us to stand on in times of uncertainty, and this book points us to that rock that will never fail us or let us down."

—JAMIE IVEY, BESTSELLING AUTHOR AND HOST OF
***THE HAPPY HOUR WITH JAMIE IVEY* PODCAST**

we go on

Finding Purpose in All of Life's Sorrows and Joys

JOHN ONWUCHEKWA

ZONDERVAN®

ZONDERVAN

We Go On

© 2022 by John Onwuchekwa

Requests for information should be addressed to:
Zondervan, *3900 Sparks Dr. SE, Grand Rapids, Michigan 49546*

ISBN 978-0-310-46011-4
ISBN 978-0-310-46015-2 (audiobook)
ISBN 978-0-310-46014-5 (eBook)

Art direction and cover design: Tiffany Forrester
Interior design: Emily Ghattas

The opening image on the introduction, as well as the pictures provided on
  pages XII-XII, XV, 2, and 56–57 were provided courtesy of Erin Fender.
The picture on page 28 was provided courtesy of Brian Renshaw.
The picture on page 40 was provided courtesy of Rikki Brew.

Printed in China

22 23 24 25 26 DSC 10 9 8 7 6 5 4 3 2 1

To CJ, Alaya, and Asher:
I hope one day you read these words
with pride and live with the purpose
your dad deposited into so many of us.

contents

The words of the Teacher, son
of David, king in Jerusalem:
"Meaningless! Meaningless!" says
the Teacher. "Utterly meaningless!
Everything is meaningless."

ECCLESIASTES 1:1–2

confessions

Reading these words lifted me out of my depression. *For real!* I know it sounds like I'm just trying to hook you early, but I'm serious. Hear me out. Hear *him* out. It's January 2016. I'm in the parking lot of Lenox Mall in Atlanta, white-knuckled behind a steering wheel, and I'm heated! I've just come back from doing a chapel service at the University of Georgia for the Texas A&M men's basketball team. Before I know it I find myself cussing out some kids who have taken my parking spot, seamlessly stringing phrases together like you do when you recite your favorite song lyrics. My fluency shocked me. Definitely not a good look for a pastor. What makes it worse is that after I finish my little tantrum, a space opens up right next to the one

I lost. But still. This isn't me. Something is off. Something really big.

On April 14, 2015, not even a year earlier, my world crumbled. I still remember it clearly—dragging myself into the morgue with my mom and dad. And there was my brother, my *perfect* brother, horizontal and stiff in the cool light, laid out on that cold matte gray table. It's crazy the things you remember. The horsefly buzzing like an electric shaver. My dad, weeping.

My brother Sam was a model son to his parents, Nigerian immigrants who gave it all to provide a better life for their kids. He was the most determined and self-sacrificial person I've ever known. He was a brilliant student, a talented athlete. He kept out of trouble and avoided troublesome people like they were contagious. When he got mad to the point of cussing, the words seldom came out. But when they did they *always* sounded borrowed, ill-fitting, like they belonged to someone else. He had a wife and three loving kids, ages five, three, and one. And there he was—thirty-two years old, in the prime of his life, and no one, not a single medical professional, could figure out why he died. It didn't make sense. It was just *meaningless*.

When Sam went, I went with him. I changed overnight. I used to be the kind of guy who always looked on the bright side, whose bad days could be counted on one hand. But after my brother died, I was just searching for shadows. My resentment grew, my hopelessness deepened, and apathy surrounded me.

Did I mention we were slated to start a new church six weeks after he died? All that was heavy, but the months would keep piling on stuff for me to carry. Emmanuel, my older brother, had come down to Atlanta to reconnect. Let's just say he and Sam had lived very different lives. And I hated him for it. We used to be the best of friends, but when I was young and needed him most, he was out in the streets *doing* the most. By the time he came back in my life, I was as bitter and calloused as I was insecure. Trying to prove I didn't need him. I had lost so much time with him. And then he moved back to Atlanta, trying to rekindle a relationship that had lost its spark a long time ago. *Why was he here, needing me to take care of him, when Sam wasn't?* Honestly, y'all, it was only easy to hate Emmanuel because of how much I hated myself for already asking the question. But that's how it was. I was broken. I just didn't know how badly.

> When Sam went, I went with him. His death changed me overnight.

The day before the church's preview service—five weeks after Sam's death—my wife, Shawndra, and I got into *perhaps one of the worst* arguments of our marriage.

It's crazy the things
you remember,
the important
and the trivial.

It's crazy th
things yo
mbe
ortar
d th
trivia

What about? I can't remember. She can't either. But that's how things go, isn't it? The size of the fight rarely reflects the size of the problem. This time, though, I didn't care. I'd lost all desire to fight for her. I'd lost all desire to fight for us. She said she was leaving, and the words *let me help you pack* fell violently from my lips. If it wasn't for our closest people coming around, we would have been in real trouble. Not knowing how to deal with the seemingly meaningless loss of my brother was tearing my life apart. I didn't know what to do with myself, and no one else knew either.

Fast-forward a few months to March 2016. I began a much-needed sabbatical—a time of rest, a time for healing. Shawndra and I had moved into a new house, and some friends of mine had helped transform what had been a worn-down, dusty workspace into a study. I affectionately refer to it as "The Shed." And that's where I found Ecclesiastes. Or Ecclesiastes found me.

I've heard someone say that while the rest of the Bible speaks *to* us, the Psalms speak *for* us. Well, I believe you can say something similar about Ecclesiastes. It cries *with* us in our sorrow, in our disappointment. It shares with us in our pain and frustration. It doesn't give easy answers to difficult questions. It sees things as they really are. But it also doesn't leave you there. It didn't leave *me* there.

Here's what I mean. Misery loves company, and in the

Life is best shared with the people you love.

opening pages of the book, I found the company my misery was looking for. It was refreshing to find someone else who felt the utter meaninglessness of the world. It was *shocking* to realize that the man who wrote Ecclesiastes, a guy I call "the Teacher," got to the same conclusion by traveling down such a different road. I arrived at my conclusion after feeling like I'd *lost it all*. He *had it all* and realized life was meaningless. For the first time I realized that maybe meaning isn't found in a particular destination or set of circumstances. Maybe purpose and peace are found in something different altogether.

Ecclesiastes comes to us in the words of the Teacher—someone who had seen and done it all. Hear me out, Fam: I've seen a lot, especially as a pastor, but my life experience pales in comparison to his. However, what I *can* do is share with you my experience of living with and learning from the Teacher. I want to show you that being honest about the seeming meaninglessness of our present joys and sorrows isn't the same as being hopeless about the future. Honesty and hope aren't parallel streets we travel down. They intersect. Which means we don't have to choose if we're going to be honest or hopeful. We can live at the intersection. We can be both. In fact, understanding what really matters today—or what really doesn't matter—has real consequences for the way you'll live your life tomorrow, and the next day, and the day after that.

But what if you aren't at rock bottom? What if, like me before all this went down, everything is on the up and up? Is there something here for you? Absolutely. Remember, the Teacher had everything. He'd seen everything. So, even if you're already at the top rung of the corporate ladder, some old head enjoying the fruits of your labor, or a sixteen-year-old with a full tank of gas ready to hit the road, this is for you. Because it is about where you go next, where *we* go next, and what we do with the knowledge we've gained along the way. Hopeless, hopeful, or somewhere in between, aren't these the questions on everybody's mind: *Where do we go from here, and how do we use what we've learned so far?* Aren't these the questions we all want answered?

So, come in! Make yourself at home. Get comfortable. In the coming pages, we're going to talk about finding purpose in life through the lens of Ecclesiastes. We're going to hear about the things we think are important—whether it's love, respect, knowledge, or work—and how we should see them for what they are and for what they're not.

There's nothing too small to address, nothing too sacred to completely undress. My life, at least for the purpose of this topic, is an open book. But I just want to warn you, the pages are made of glass— they're very fragile. I'm trusting you with them. Handle them with care. Take this book for what it is, and don't put too much weight on those pages; they'll shatter underneath the weight of expectations they were never meant

> Life is about where you go next, where *we* go next, and what we do with the knowledge we've gained along the way.

to carry. On these glass pages, I offer short insights on finding purpose in and through some of the most important aspects of life—our work, our pursuits of knowledge and pleasure and money and security, and everything in between. I hope you see yourself in some of my reflections on life and finding purpose in it.

This is a short book on how I kept moving.

Not only was the Teacher

wise, but he also imparted

knowledge to the people.

ECCLESIASTES 12:9

teach me

First up, let's meet the Teacher, and then we'll make our way through the most important observations and lessons of his book on life, Ecclesiastes. After that, we'll apply his wisdom to some of life's foremost pursuits— things like knowledge, pleasure, work, money, adversity. We'll also explore what he has to say about keeping your sanity while fighting for change, and how looking at death helps us see life more clearly.

Before we meet the Teacher, though, let's chat more generally about teachers. I'm not concerned mainly with ones that lecture in classrooms, sit behind desks, and give grades. I mean the people in our lives we look up to, learn

Experience isn't the best teacher. Someone else's is. You get to learn the same lesson without experiencing the same heartache.

from, and lean on to help us move through life. Truth is, we're always learning from others no matter how independent we think we are. Because even though experience is a great teacher, sometimes someone else's experience is a *better* teacher. If we pay attention to their words and example, we can learn the same lesson while saving ourselves a lot of heartache. That was true of me and my brother Sam. He was my teacher.

Let's turn the clock back to Southwest Houston, 1997, and I'll show you what I mean. Those were the days of Puffy and Mase in shiny suits. Sam and I had shiny suits too. Ours were just reserved for church on Sunday. On Friday and Saturday nights, though, you'd find us with the homies at FunPlex (it was our skating rink of choice at the time), living for the two most important words of the weekend: *couples skate*. That's when we'd try our luck with the ladies. It was hilarious. We celebrated when they said yes. We clowned each other about the creative ways they said no. Sam didn't get many nos. He knew what he was doing. Me? Not so much.

You heard about the designated chip holder? He's the guy who stays behind and watches the nachos and drinks while the homies take the girls for a spin. That was me, sitting alone in the mirror ball light. Boyz II Men's "I'll Make Love to You" would be crooning through the speakers, but I'd be off in the corner *living* Brian McKnight's

"One Last Cry." Or, that *was* me, until I finally pulled Sam aside.

Sam always knew the answers. He said, *Listen, bro. When you roll up and ask her to skate, don't cold call her, bro. No one likes a telemarketer. Introduce yourself. Say hi. Shake her hand, establish some friendly contact. Give her a compliment.* And the dimes didn't stop there. *If she says yes, make sure to keep those palms dry. And if you can't, skate backward. That way you only need to touch her fingertips while still keeping eye contact.* Gold. Pure gold.

Who are we learning from and why? Who are *your* teachers?

And naturally, Sam's wisdom transcended the skating rink. The older we grew, the more I learned from him. College? Buying a car? Becoming a homeowner? In each and every situation, he saw the big picture, knew how the game was played, and was more than willing to just *give away* his trade secrets. He taught me so much I could've never worked out on my own. That was one of the reasons his passing was so hard. I didn't just lose a brother. I lost my teacher.

Sam's absence made me think not only about where I was going to go next but also who was going to help show me the way.

Truth be told, there's a lot of options out there. The

teach me

situation isn't helped either when there is a profit to be made. Bookstores have shelves bursting with books boasting expertise on one subject or another. You want to learn to be successful in business, in the kitchen, in the bedroom? *Here's what you need to know.*

And online? It's a whole other world. Podcasts, master classes, social media influencers. There is something for everyone on just about anything. The louder, the more persuasive the voice, the better-looking the speaker, the more we pay attention. And you can curate it all. Whatever you want—whether or not you really need it, whether or not it's even good for you.

I don't know how we keep it all straight. But we need to. 'Cause we are all watching and listening. Even if we think we're going it alone, we are all learning. The question is: Who are we learning from and why? Who are *your* teachers?

What's Your Story?

So, hold up a minute. Let me ask you a few questions:

- Who are you listening to? Who are you reading?

- Check your shelf, your bedside table, your phone, your YouTube history and suggestions. Who has your attention? And why?
- Think about the last major decision you made. It could be who you dated, what job you took, or where you moved. Just pick one.
- Think about who most influenced you in making that decision. Think about why you listened to them and not someone else.
- Reflect. What does this tell you about what you value most in your teachers?

A TEACHER WITH RECEIPTS

So, we're surrounded by teachers, right? Some we seek out; others are flagging us down. But who is *this* teacher, the Teacher of Ecclesiastes, and why is he worth listening to? What has he got to offer that you can't just find somewhere else or figure out yourself?

The Teacher. We actually don't know who he is for sure, but he's introduced in the book as if he's Solomon, the ancient Israelite king of Jerusalem.

In the Bible, Solomon is famous for his wisdom. There's a story where God appears to him in a dream and tells him to ask for whatever he wants. Instead of seeking a long life, wealth, or the death of his enemies, Solomon asks for wisdom. God is so pleased with Solomon's response that He not only gives him what he asks—unrivaled wisdom—but also unimaginable wealth and honor.

And so Solomon became one of the most accomplished and privileged kings in all of human history. Imagine someone with the wealth of Warren Buffet, the business sense and savvy of Jay-Z, sprinkled with the prestige of Oprah, and topped off with the power and respect of your favorite president. He's all that and more. And this rings true of the Teacher in Ecclesiastes. Not only does he have great wisdom, but he has access to anything and everything under the sun.

Whoever the Teacher is in Ecclesiastes, he wants Solomon's reputation to come to mind when you read the book. It's either Solomon or someone who has a PhD in Solomon. This Teacher has a wealth of experience that he's spending on educating you.

So, when it comes to giving out advice, the Teacher's qualified. He's got the experience and authority to speak on what he knows—which is really the stuff *you want to know*. This ain't someone who can't get a date writing to you about the benefits of *loving yourself*. This ain't someone

7

who's broke telling you *there's more to life than money.* He's the most eligible bachelor. Forget being in the wealthiest one percentile; his portfolio places him in the top one-hundredth of a percentile. Simply put, he's lived the life of *your* dreams.

Now, if someone like that was going to write a book, what are the first words you'd expect to read? Maybe, *All right, if you really want to make money, here's where to invest!* or *Let me tell you how to find success in between the sheets!* or *If you want to leave a lasting impact, follow these twelve steps!* But that's not how it starts at all. Instead, it's *Meaningless! Meaningless!* I get it. It sounds crazy. But it's true, and in the next chapter, we are going talk about why.

> The Teacher has the experience and authority to speak on what he knows—the stuff you want to know.

Can we trust someone who says something like this? Yeah, but we need to set a little context. Solomon is just as famous for his fall from grace. As time went by, he stopped living by his ideals. He sought satisfaction in the wrong places, abused his power, and lost his connection with God—the source of every good thing he had been given.

Solomon wasn't the first, and he definitely wasn't the last to lose his way. But when our teachers and leaders fail

teach me

8

us, it disorients us. It shakes our confidence. We become disillusioned, bitter, and angry. And when trust is broken, it's really hard, if not impossible, to rebuild.

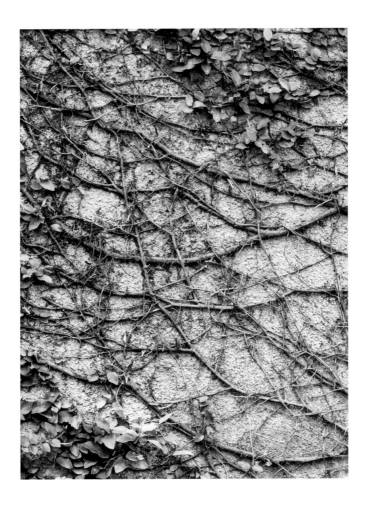

FAILURE: AN UNLIKELY TEACHER

Have you had a teacher or leader fail you? Did you invest so much into that person, only to find that it was wasted?

For my part, I've got countless stories. The one that comes to mind, though, happened in the late fall of 2011. I'm stuck to the leather couch in the basement of my place in Atlanta—the fruits of following Sam's advice on all things real estate. Then my phone buzzes on my leg. It's a friend from high school. He's crying—I can literally hear the teardrops hitting the receiver on his end. I can't believe what he's saying, so I put him on speakerphone and scroll to the front page of the newspaper. I recognize the picture immediately. Those stern, beady eyes, full of conviction. One of our high school coaches. He had killed himself after it came out he'd been fooling around with one of his students. He was the one who always preached integrity. And there he was, the very guy he warned me not to become.

So, what's your story? I'm sure you've had a similar experience, or at least know somebody who has. Take a moment and reflect on how a teacher's failure hit you and how you responded. Is there anything you wish you could have said to him or her? Take a moment. Put it into words. You can say it out loud, or you can put it on the page. Let it out.

Come Together

When you're ready, pray with me.

> Lord,
>
> Heal my wounds. Heal my resentments. Help me trust, even when others have broken that trust. Help me learn from the mistakes of others, even when they have hurt me. In Your mercy, prevent me from making the same mistakes. And if I have made those mistakes, forgive me as I seek the forgiveness of others.
>
> In Your mercy,
>
> Amen.

At some point my old coach started hiding. But our secrets get tired of playing hide-and-go-seek. Eventually, they spring up from their hiding spot and shout, *"Here I am!"* And my coach got found out.

Here's what makes the Teacher so different. He doesn't make us play hide-and-go-seek with his flaws. He shows us where they're hiding before they show themselves. In

Ecclesiastes he's drawn the curtains back on his life, and it's all there—his flaws and failings—for everyone to see. There are no trade secrets. There's no personal brand or corporate sponsorship to maintain. He isn't even trying to sell you anything.

He's giving out his wisdom for free to anyone who will listen. Well, *free* for us. He paid a hefty price.

'Cause when we listen to the Teacher, we aren't catching someone on a high. He's not offering platitudes about how great life is when you're at the top without a care in the world. He's come down. He's sober. And he wants you to be too. It's not about being sad or disappointed in life—though the Teacher definitely has regrets. It's about clarity. It's about seeing things for what they truly are. The Teacher wants you to find the life you want by enjoying the life you have. And he wants you to learn from his mistakes, so you won't go chasing after stuff like money, pleasure, and knowledge, expecting them to satisfy you. He already got more of that than he could ever need, and it was a dead end, a waste of time. He wants to save you from the heartache. *I* want to save you from the heartache. So, come, let's sit at the feet of the Teacher and learn together. But first, let's pray together.

Find the life you want by enjoying the life you have.

Heavenly Father,

You reserve wisdom for the humble. Tear down the walls of pride and defensiveness that surround us. Help us listen and learn. Use the Teacher and this book, I pray, to help us grow in wisdom and purpose. Guide us, hold us up, and bring us to You!

Amen.

I have seen all the things

that are done under the sun;

all of them are meaningless,

a chasing after the wind.

ECCLESIASTES 1:14

daydream

Put your face in the dirt or we'll shoot!

I'm seventeen years old, somewhere in the middle of Nigeria, and automatic rifles are pointed at my head. I press my face so hard against the ground, the rocks almost break my skin. Dust is everywhere. My shoulders contract and release at the thud of every bag as it hits the ground. I hear the sound of my family's muffled cries as they plead for mercy—mercy from the gunmen, mercy from God. *Please, Lord, help us.*

I've never held hands with fear like that before or since. But even as my body lay there, shaking, preparing for the worst, my mind was miles away. You know how people talk about their life flashing before their eyes? Well, something like that happened to me. Only it wasn't so much the life I lived; it was the life I hoped to live. I could see it vanish.

15

In the cloud of dust, shouting, and tears, I had a sudden clarity. Even though I was afraid to die, there was something I feared more—that I had wasted my life.

Up until that point, everything was going according to plan. We'd been driving down the road, and I'd been staring out the window. I really wasn't looking outside though. I was looking ahead. In a few weeks' time I'd be back in the States, seeing (who I thought was) the girl of my dreams. I'd be going to college and playing ball with my bigger brother.

One bullet could have taken it all away.

One bullet still can.

MAYBE THERE'S MORE THAN THIS

One of my favorite Jay-Z songs is "This Can't Be Life." I love how he looks at the world in that song—so full of danger, so full of sudden loss—and protests the life he's come to know. It can't be this fragile or this fickle. *It can't be.* And I get what he's saying. But he's wrong.

In Ecclesiastes, the Teacher tells us this *is* life. And until you see it for what it really is, you'll never see it clearly. You're daydreaming. You'll live in denial, searching for stability in things made of smoke. You'll try to find satisfaction in what can never truly satisfy. And sooner or later, you'll find it's all meaningless, a chasing after the wind.

The word *meaningless* in Ecclesiastes is a translation from the Hebrew *hebel*. It literally means "breath or vapor." It's also where we get the name *Abel*. Abel, who is described in the book of Genesis, is the innocent son of Adam and Eve. But he is brutally and irrationally murdered by his older brother, Cain. He's the only innocent one in the family, yet he's the first to die (and the only one to die so violently). His life was nothing but a breath, a vapor—as meaningless as his death. So, when the Teacher says our lives are *hebel*, he's basically saying they are like Abel. Even when they are at their best, they can be snatched away like *that*.

But maybe you're not convinced. Maybe you don't see things that way. You've got goals of your own and a plan

Even though I was afraid to die, there was something I feared more—that I had wasted my life.

for your life. Maybe you believe your plan and God's plan are one and the same. Or maybe they'll overlap eventually. You've read the Teacher's perspective on life and don't pay him any mind. He seems like the grizzled old head barking at the kids to *get off his lawn!* So, tune the Teacher out. Hope that things won't break that way for you. Believe you'll be the exception.

Just wait. All it takes is one day, one mistake, one accident—it doesn't even have to be yours. Then everything will change. I thought I had my whole life ahead of me. I was living in the future tense. All my grinding, my hustle, was going to pay off. But on that dirt road in Nigeria, my life could have been gone in a *breath.*

Breathe

I'm sure you've also had your fair share of close calls. Think about how those experiences have shaped you, how they've changed your perspective. Maybe you had a brush with death that left you promising never to take life for granted. Have you kept that promise?

The Teacher comes at it from a different perspective. He isn't like seventeen-year-old John O. He's not looking through the windshield at what lies ahead. He's looking in the rearview mirror. He's not hoping for success. He's reflecting on accomplishments. And here's the thing: all that he gained, every accomplishment, every dollar, every notch on the bedpost—none of it amounted to much of anything. He had more regrets than accomplishments. Pleasure? Empty. Wealth? Vapor. Work? Meaningless. You may call it depressing or self-defeating. But you have to respect his clarity. He sees it for what it is.

My clarity came from a near-death experience at a young age. The Teacher's clarity came from a lifetime's experience at an old age. Yet we arrived at the same conclusion: everything you're striving for, everything you're hoping for, they aren't going to satisfy like you think they will. And that's life. You know it's true. Think of everything you've collected along the way to what you're hoping to become. You *know* you can't take it with you once you're gone, but you collect it anyway.

The Teacher says, *Everyone comes naked from their mother's womb, and as everyone comes, so they depart. They take nothing from their toil that they can carry in their hands* (Ecclesiastes 5:15).

You work and work and work for all this *stuff.* You worry about it. You lose sleep over it. You sacrifice relationships for it. Maybe you lash out when people seem to threaten it. Maybe you still believe that somehow, maybe, it's going to satisfy you, that it's going to answer some deep question within you. And yet you still know that wherever it's going in the end, it ain't going with you. Car collecting. Card collecting. Stock collecting. Shoe collecting. Book collecting. Record collecting. As an old head once said to me, it's all just "wind collecting." Chasing after the wind.

What's Your Story?

Let's try some accounting.

- Think about the most expensive thing you bought in the past year. What does it say to you about what you really value?
- Reflect on your goals. Where are you heading? Are you so focused on the future that you're losing track of what's going on *right now*?
- Take your mental temperature. What's stressing you out? It could be something at home or at work. Maybe it's something that keeps you up at night. Why does it matter to you? Should it?

I know this is tough to come to grips with, but you need to see yourself clearly. You need to know what you really value and what you're really chasing after. These things can rule your life if you let them. But do they satisfy?

Father,
> *Give me the eyes to see the truth. I don't want to lie to myself. I don't want to chase after things that will never satisfy. Give me courage to choose another path. A better one.*
>
> *Amen.*

When the Teacher realized that everything he'd pursued turned out to be meaningless, he found he hated life. And not just life, but everything he'd devoted his life to—all the accomplishments, all the *stuff.*

It's understandable. Unmet expectations can breed resentment. Unfulfilled hope often sprouts into beanstalks of bitterness. When God's plans and our plans diverge, we have a crisis of faith. We get angry with God, with others, even with ourselves. And maybe, just maybe, we start to wonder if life really is worth living. Maybe we find that we hate life too.

Do you feel that way? I've felt that way. And that's how the Teacher felt. He lost hope. Until he received a deeper revelation:

> This is what I have observed to be good: that it is appropriate for a person to eat, to drink and to find satisfaction in their toilsome labor under the sun during the few days of life God has given them—for this is their lot. Moreover, when God gives someone wealth and possessions and the ability to enjoy them, to accept their lot and be happy in their toil—this is a gift of God. They seldom reflect on the days of their life, because God keeps them occupied with gladness of heart.
>
> **Ecclesiastes 5:18–20**

There's a lot here we'll talk about later, but right now, let's focus on *this moment*.

ACCEPT THE BITTER WITH THE SWEET

It's God's gift to live in the *present*. This doesn't fix everything. There's still toil. And trouble. And disappointment. But instead of expecting more from life than it could possibly give, you receive this day from the hand of God and enjoy it in the moment. *This moment.* Bitterness and sweetness together. All of it is a gift.

Here's what I mean. Take a cup of coffee—the kind I'd give you while we're clothed in the shade of my Atlanta porch, our ears tickled by my mostly '90s R & B playlist. Now take your time. Inhale the aroma. Feel the warmth. Swirl it in the cup. Pay attention to how it sticks to the sides and slips off. Take a sip. Slowly. Now catch this: expect the bitterness; wait for the sweetness. Notice the subtlety of its flavor. It's all there, and it's a gift to enjoy.

Coffee is complex. Only novices, people who haven't really been acquainted with it, describe it as bitter. And it *is* bitter; there's no denying that. But that's not all it is. There's so much more to enjoy if you embrace the coffee's bitterness and look for something else.

Hear me out! All I'm saying is that there's a lot to miss out on if (1) you're so determined *not* to taste the coffee's bitterness that you mask it with cream, sugar, milk, or anything sweet at your disposal; or (2) you only drink it as a means to an end—using the caffeine to help you accomplish some other task you feel is more important than the enjoyment awaiting you in that cup.

A lot of folks treat life like a cup of coffee. They don't want to taste the bitterness. They even want to pretend it isn't there. So, they reach for accomplishments, relationships, and work—anything to make life *sweeter,* or at least less bitter. And before they know it, life becomes the equivalent of a "coffee-flavored" beverage. It's not really life, like it's not really coffee. It's just "life-flavored." They want it sweet or not at all.

But why shouldn't you just choose to mask the bitterness? What are you really missing? Fullness of life. Complexity. Uniqueness of flavor. Story. History. Homeland. This isn't me just trying to sell you on coffee—I want to sell you on a different way to see life.

So, what about those who only see coffee as a means to an end? They don't care about the flavor; they care about the caffeine. That's like living in the future tense. It's always the next thing. And the sweeter it goes down, the better— that way you don't have to pay too much attention to it. It doesn't distract you. It just gets you where you want to go. But that's not life either. That's out of touch with the present. That's missing out on the gift.

Coffee, like life, is about receiving the bitterness and the sweetness together. It demands patience. In fact, my friend Joe once told me that coffee has helped him *slow down*. To brew it properly means *not* watching your clock on the way to somewhere else; it means paying attention and enjoying the experience in that very moment. *This* moment.

Your lot in life, to use the Teacher's words, is to enjoy the cup of coffee in your hands. Expecting the bitterness

27

Coffee, like life, is about
receiving the bitterness
and the sweetness together.

to come, but not staying there. Coffee is bitter, but it's much more than that. Bitterness and sweetness aren't like oil and water. As the Teacher says, it is God who makes things meaningful. He is the One who gives wealth and possessions and the ability to enjoy and accept them. While spending our time chasing what could be, we miss out on enjoying what is. We never even consider that the joy we often forfeit in the present (in hopes of seeking more) is more than enough to satisfy us. But to live in the present tense, to pay attention to what is before you and to accept that life is both bitter and sweet? That's a blessing. Like my second chance at life after Nigeria, like that cup of Ethiopian coffee on my porch in Atlanta, it is a gift from God.

Let's pray.

Father,

I don't want to spend my life chasing after the wind. I don't want to get so caught up in my future plans that I miss the gift of the present, the gift of this moment. Help me slow down. Help me trust You. Help me wait for the subtle sweetness of life even if all I can taste right now is its bitterness.

Amen.

There is a time for everything,

and a season for every

activity under the heavens.

ECCLESIASTES 3:1

it's about time

Shawndra and I got married in 2007, right out of college. We were babies, but that didn't stop us wanting to make some of our own right away. Some folks think it best to enjoy one another for a while. To let each other's company settle in the garden of marriage before adding new blooms to the family. *Take your time. There's plenty of time for babies and diapers and strollers,* they told us. *You've got careers to grow, places to go. See the world, save some money, and then have kids when you're done with that.*

Some people don't want kids at all. Others don't have much of a choice one way or another.

We were the others.

As I write, it's been fourteen years since we first started trying. We have yet to conceive.

When our marriage was young and new, it was, *Don't worry, your time will come.* Those days and months swelled

31

into years. Different doctors came back with the same statements. *Nothing's wrong.* Normally, those words from a doctor are enough to release the knots from tense shoulders. When it comes to the reason for infertility, *nothing's wrong* isn't bittersweet. It's sweetly bitter. A taste that ages on your tongue.

Initially it's sweet. You begin each month *pregnant with hope.* Four weeks later, you're disappointed but not completely deflated. You refill your hope by repeating the words, *Not yet; it's just not yet.* You begin the next month full of hope, a little less full than before, but full nonetheless. Then the sweetness sours. As the months mature into your first decade of marriage, you realize the words *not yet* were novocaine. They only delayed the sting of the words *not ever.*

SEASONS WE DON'T WANT

In the last chapter we talked about what we hope will satisfy us. We can have our whole lives planned out—and then something happens. We find that our plans were like chasing wind. But what about when you feel you're the only one missing out? You look around, and it seems like everything is falling into place for everybody else. Marriage leads to children leads to grandchildren and on it goes. Or maybe it's something else. Your friends have gone from high school to college to a good job to homeownership. And you're stuck somewhere in between, floundering while they're crossing finish lines. You've been told, *Don't worry, your time will come.* You're still waiting.

But what if your plans have worked out, only they've worked out too well? You know what it's like to be depressed in a valley, but you're depressed on a mountaintop. You're not as satisfied as you thought you'd be, and now you're stuck in a life you don't want. The season seems endless.

As Shawn and I struggled with our infertility, we'd have friends come to our house seeking counsel for the exact opposite reason. They were getting too pregnant, too often. The long nine months, complications, and extra mouths to feed felt like a burden, not a blessing. As we sought to remind others of the great gift of life—no matter how hard it might seem in the present—we were privately grieving. Our friends were desperate for that season to end. We were desperate for it to begin.

In Ecclesiastes 3:2–8, the Teacher describes the many seasons of life:

> a time to be born and a time to die,
> a time to plant and a time to uproot,
> a time to weep and a time to laugh,
> a time to mourn and a time to dance,
> . . . and so on.

Take a close look at the times outlined here. Which of those seasons did they *actually* want to happen? A time to die, as well as a time to be born? A time to mourn, as well as a time to dance? I doubt they were hoping for both. They wanted the good times, not the bad. And so do we. But as Shawn and I have found out, and the Teacher learned long before, the seasons are just as likely to be hard. The coming change may not be a good one.

Breathe

We're all in seasons of life. Sometimes it helps just to know which one we're in. So, where are you at right now?

Read back over Ecclesiastes 3:2–8. Where do you see yourself in those verses? Maybe you're in the planting season. You're thinking about the future. There is hope. But there is also anxiety. You don't know what the harvest will bring. Or maybe you're in an uprooting season. You're moving to a new city. You're leaving a relationship. There's something in your life that needs to go. Whatever it is, ask God for guidance.

> *Father,*
>
> *In Your mercy, show me the season I'm in. Help me acknowledge it for what it is, even if it's hard. Remind me that even if things are going really well right now, it's only a season. It will pass. Help me see Your purposes at work no matter the time or season. Whether life is good or bad, easy or difficult, or it just seems*

> *stuck, may my hope, faith, and love grow in You more deeply.*
>
> *Amen.*

RELEASE YOUR GRIP
AND FIND PEACE

When the Teacher tells us there is a time to weep and a time to laugh, he's not talking about options. You can't just add the seasons of life you prefer to your life's registry. He's saying life is weeping *and* laughing, tearing *and* mending, keeping *and* throwing away. And when he tells us there is a time for everything, he's not offering some wise and optimistic sentiment. He's saying that *there is nothing new under the sun.* The cycle always repeats, one season always follows another, and there isn't anything you can do to change it.

The Teacher's wisdom helped him discern the seasons of life; it didn't free him. The seasons constrained him like everyone else. The difference is, he knew he wasn't in control. And this enabled him to face and embrace each season as it came.

This is ancient wisdom. Through most of human history, and even in large parts of the world today, people have lived close to the land. They've labored in the fields; they've looked after herds and flocks. Their lives have been governed by the seasons, the cycles of planting and harvesting, and the phases of the moon. The Teacher doesn't have to explain to them that there's a time for everything. They already know.

But for those of us living in the modern world? We might need more help. That's because we've been doing our best, through technological advancement, to break the cycle of life's seasons. And in some ways, we seem to have almost done it. Refrigeration slows the process of decay. Injections slow the appearance of aging. Birth control stops a biological cycle in its tracks. And we believe the best is still ahead. But like the great philosopher Brandy Norwood famously said, *Almost doesn't count!*

Maybe that's why we are often so discontent. No matter how hard we try, the seasons still change. We try to make summer last forever, but then the leaves start to fall and there's nothing our shorts, shades, jackets, or heated blankets can do about it. You can't change the weather by changing your wardrobe, just as you can't escape death by taking your vitamins.

That's the bad news. Now here's the good. Spring always follows winter. Troubles and tribulations, however

Knowing he wasn't in control enabled the Teacher to embrace every season.

hard they may be, are only temporary. Take this to heart, and you won't get too high or too low, depending on the season. You'll find the ability to live in the tension. Instead of fighting against the change, you'll learn to accept the inevitable. You'll find peace.

And here's some more good news. Actually, it's way better than that: You're not in control; God is. And seeing your life in the light of that truth is going to set you free.

You heard of the Copernican revolution? In the sixteenth century, this dude Copernicus came up with the radical idea that the earth wasn't the center of the universe, but revolved around the sun. People thought he was crazy. After all, they saw the sun rise and set each day even as they stood still. But we know better now. Why? Because we've got a better perspective. We know the truth. We need a Copernican revolution for our hearts.

Spring always follows winter.

Why? Because we still act as if we're at the center of the universe. But like the earth, we're actually the ones in motion, always moving from one season into the next. We circle a much greater center, a center we could not hope to live without. And that center is God. We need that perspective. Joy is found *on* the journey, not *in* a destination.

GET REAL

Your life is going to continue to spin out of control if you try to put anything or anyone else at its center. Find your orbit around God. You might find it hard at first. People may look at you sideways. But it's going to bring you freedom—freedom from self-centeredness, freedom from orienting yourself around things that won't satisfy, and freedom from the burden of unmet expectations about how your life is supposed to turn out. You don't need to know where you're going if you know that God does.

Come Together

Father,

I want You to be the center of my life. I know the universe doesn't revolve around me. Help me accept that knowledge joyfully and live with the comfort it brings. Change my perspective. Direct my path away from the pursuits that will never satisfy. Give me the freedom that only You can give. You are in control.

Amen.

You're not in control, and that's some
of the best news you've heard all day.

A TIME TO WEEP, A TIME TO LAUGH

But God isn't just the center of our existence; He's the Controller. The Author. He doesn't just watch our seasons, whether easy or difficult, from afar. He chooses to make them meaningful, even beautiful. For as the Teacher tells us, *He has made everything beautiful in its time* (3:11). Let me show you how I know that's true.

It has been fourteen years, and Shawn and I still haven't conceived.

But there's something I haven't told you. We have a daughter!

On April 10, 2015, almost eight years since Shawn and I started trying, we got a phone call from our caseworker. *I'm so sorry, but the adoption didn't go through. I tried everything, but there's nothing left to do.* We had spent a year working and waiting, waiting, *waiting* to adopt a baby girl. And then—*a time for weeping.* That was four days before Sam passed. *A time to die.* Where's the meaning in that? Where's the beauty?

But wait. I'm not done. Two years later—to the day—we get another call. *She's yours. You can drive down and come and meet your daughter.* And we did. A little girl had been born premature less than a week earlier. When we first saw her, the tears rushed out of our eyes and fell on the incubator. They ran down the side onto the latches, like they wanted to open them up so we could hug her. She needed a breathing machine, but she was ours.

Four days later, it's Good Friday. On the day that Christians remember the suffering and death of Jesus Christ, I sit with my daughter in the hospital, reading. The book is J. I. Packer's *Knowing God*. As I'm working through the chapter on adoption, warming her against my bare chest, the doctor comes in and starts speaking really fast. I can't follow what he's saying. He is too excited, so I start to get nervous. All I hear is, *Today . . . breathe . . . her . . . let me hold her.* Before I know it, he takes her away. But before I can protest, she is back in my arms, warm against my chest—but somehow lighter. Her breathing tube is gone. On April 14, 2017, I held Ava as she breathed freely for the first time. It was two years—to the day—that Sam breathed his last. And almost two thousand years—to the day—that Jesus gave up His spirit to the Father.

I cannot make my life meaningful. I don't have that much control. But I can testify with my whole heart that *God made something beautiful in its time* when He brought Ava into our family. And He will do the same for you. In time.

This is who God is. This is what God can do. Meaning is in His hands. The seasons don't constrain Him. He loves to call the brightest futures out of the darkest circumstances. And in the death and resurrection of Jesus Christ,

He raised His Son to eternal life. He broke the cycle. And not only for Jesus—for *all* those who believe in Him, who put *Him* at the center of their lives. So, if you haven't done it already, why wait? The time is now.

Father,

No matter what season of life I am in, I am Yours. You are my center. I trust You to make my life meaningful in Your sight, even if I cannot see it. Make my life beautiful in its time. Allow me to wait hopefully.

Amen.

You cannot understand

the work of God,

the Maker of all things.

ECCLESIASTES 11:5

chapter four

what's goin' on?

Babe, you want a tuna fish sandwich?

Let me set the scene: it's 2011. Shawndra and I are in
the kitchen at our first house in Atlanta, and my world's
about to get completely turned upside down. Maybe I'm
being a bit extra, but just follow me. We've covered some
hard ground in the last few chapters, but important lessons
don't just come from serious places. Sometimes all it takes
is a tuna fish sandwich. I'm watching Shawn put a big glass
mixing bowl on the counter. The tuna fish packet comes
out. (Yeah, packet. We don't mess with the canned tuna fish
in the Onwuchekwa household. We're not the biggest fans
of the tuna fish juice at the bottom.) Now she's bringing out
green onions, celery, and relish. Next is the salt and pepper.
Crackers for her, bread for me. Now I know we're getting

close. She's reaching for those all-important secret ingredients: *[redacted]*, *[redacted]*, and the most necessary, the one thing you really can't do without, *[redacted]*. Perfect. Then, for reasons beyond my comprehension, Shawn takes out the mayonnaise.

Mayonnaise?!

I've got a bit of a confession to make. Since I was a kid, I've *loved* tuna fish sandwiches. I imagine I always will. However, I had *no idea* they involved mayonnaise. I *hate* mayonnaise. I imagine I always will. With desperation stumbling out of my mouth, I tell her, *Baby, please stop! Don't mess up this good thing we got goin'!*

Her face immediately curls into a question mark that I interpret as, *When did you become a Top Chef?*

Chill, she says. *Let me do my thing. Let me worry about what's going on here. You ain't even a cook like that* (she tells no lies).

She goes on to explain that what I view as bad and would rather avoid (mayo) is necessary if she is going to make the dish I so enjoy (tuna fish). After talking me off the ledge, she says, *It's okay not to like mayo alone, but wait until you see what happens when you combine this ingredient with other things. John, let me cook.* She finishes up and puts the mixture between the bread. All I can think about is the mayo. I put the sandwich in my mouth and take a bite, closing my eyes as if that would filter out the tastes

46

I don't like. The way the tuna greets my taste buds with a warm welcome surprises me. My palate starts singing. Before long, I'm smiling, and she has that closed-mouthed grin that's screaming, *I told you so.* The sandwich was perfect.

LET HIM COOK!

There are two morals to this story: (1) a grown man can have no idea what's in a tuna fish sandwich; and (2) most of us have no idea what's *really* going on in life. We see God, the Divine Chef, mixing up life's ingredients. We stand over His shoulder nitpicking the things He allows into our bowls. Death, infertility, heartache, depression—we can't make sense of how it all fits together. We don't know the recipe. But we're also not the cooks.

Instead, we get to watch the Divine Chef take things we don't like, even *hate,* and turn them into something amazing—like that tuna fish sandwich. *Let Him cook!*

> Most of us really have no idea what's going on in life.

Over the past couple of chapters, you have seen me behind the wheel in the parking lot, unable to deal with Sam's passing. You've seen me with a gun to my head, laid out on a dirt road. You've seen me

47

hold my daughter, Ava, no longer struggling to breathe, in my arms. So much trouble, so many tears. But you've also seen hope. You've seen restoration. You've seen my story go in unexpected directions. In my life's joys and sorrows, you've seen purpose.

I didn't come up with that purpose all by myself. I wasn't sitting alone after my big argument with Shawn, thinking, *This is all part of a bigger plan.* I wasn't waiting by the phone, looking at the calendar, thinking, *You know what would be amazing? If we welcomed a little girl to our family two years—to the day—after the last adoption failed.*

Looking back, now I understand I had only part of the recipe. A very small part. And I'm not that much of a cook anyway, so I don't know what to do with the ingredients I've been given. But God knows. God sees. The Divine Chef is in His eternal kitchen, stirring together the ingredients of our passing days. He makes the meaningless meaningful. So, as the Teacher says, *Remember your Creator* (12:1).

What's Your Story?

Let's take a minute. Have you got any of these types of stories, where you were lost and then you were found like the old song says? Can you remember them?

If you're having a hard time remembering, reach out and ask someone close to you. They can often see God's grace in your life better than you can. Maybe they could do with some reminding of God's grace in *their* lives too.

- Remember how it felt to be lost. And I mean *lost*. You didn't know where you were, let alone where you were going. And you didn't know why things had played out that way.
- Remember how it felt to be *found*. The release. The freedom. Think about the process, not just the final product. Recall the steps that got you there. What was going on behind the scenes? What had to line up just so?
- For real, though, what was the mayonnaise in that tuna fish sandwich?
- When you're ready, ask yourself what this all tells you about God—who He is, and how He loves you.

SOMETIMES YOU DON'T
HAVE THE WHOLE RECIPE

But maybe you're still lost. Remembering what God's done in the past isn't quite doing it for you in the present. You need something now. Today. You're calling out to Him. You know He sees the notifications, but it feels like He's screening your calls. Confusion, doubts, suspicions, and even—if you're completely honest—a growing resentment. *Why, God?*

It's a good, important question. People in the Bible ask it all the time. Now, you may not always like the answer you get, or even get an answer that makes sense at first. But that's life.

The Teacher tells us,

> As you do not know the path of the wind,
> or how the body is formed in a mother's womb,
> so you cannot understand the work of God,
> the Maker of all things.

Ecclesiastes 11:5

You may never see the whole picture. You may never know all that goes into the recipe. And that can be frustrating, even *infuriating.* When things are going badly and you feel cut out of the loop, your *Why, God?* can easily turn into, *How could You, God? How dare You, God?!* But these are no longer questions. They're accusations. Your heart rages, and God becomes the target.

Is there a better way to respond?

I'm reminded of the story of Job. Job was a righteous man who honored God. He had great wealth, a happy family, and everything seemed to be going well. Then, without warning, it was all taken in the worst sort of ways—quickly

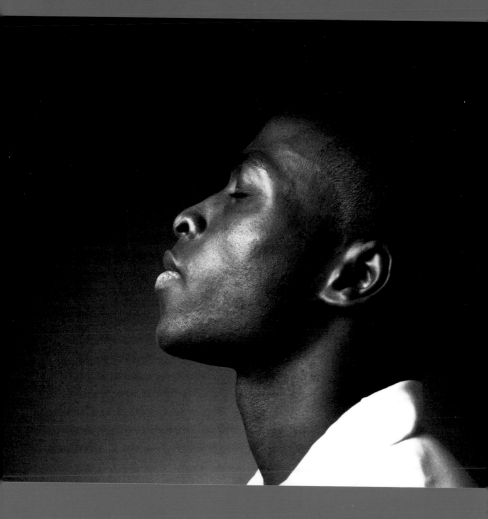

When things are going badly, it's easy to blame
God, but there's another way to respond.

and completely. He lost everything in the amount of time it takes you to read the first chapter of his story aloud. When we read Job's story, we're told ahead of time that his faith is going to be tested by suffering. Satan wants to prove to God that Job only honors Him because Job is prosperous. But no one fills Job in. His so-called friends think that he's somehow to blame, but they don't know what they're talking about. So, Job cries out to God for answers, only to get an unexpected reply. God tells Job, more or less, to know his place, to remember his Creator: *"Who is this that obscures my plans with words without knowledge?"* (Job 38:2). God may as well have said, *Let Me cook!* Job ends up proving Satan wrong and receives back everything he had lost and more. But he still isn't given any answers.

You aren't promised any answers either. And maybe that's difficult to swallow. But have you considered that your frustration, anger, and sense of injustice all come from God in the first place? I mean, if everything under the sun is all there is, if everything really is meaningless, why are you even complaining? Why should you expect anything else?

But that's the thing. Something deep within you *whispers* that life should be better, that things *do* have value. Injustice riles you up. And where else could that feeling

Deep within you there are whispers that there is something better.

come from, other than being created by a just and loving God?

The Teacher tells us that God has *set eternity in the human heart* (Ecclesiastes 3:11). And it is that eternity that makes us so unsatisfied with the present. We aren't lost because God hasn't bothered to find us. We're lost because we're determined to look for lasting purpose in passing things. Stop staring at the ingredients, trying to figure out how they all fit together. Look to the Chef.

Breathe

So, what now? How do you go on from here? One word: worship.

Reflect for a moment on what worship means to you. Does it bring you joy? Does it make you uncomfortable? Are you even sure what it is?

Sometimes when we're in a hard season, the last thing we want to do is worship. Why do you think that is?

I want you to consider that worship might actually be *the* most important thing you can do when you are in the midst of suffering.

54

CLOSED MOUTH, OPEN EARS

Our frustration with life can lead us to focus increasingly on ourselves. We need to turn our attention, instead, to our Creator. And that's what worship does. It affirms who He is and where we stand before Him. The Teacher recognized this, and we need to as well.

He says, *Guard your steps when you go to the house of God. Go near to listen rather than to offer the sacrifice of fools, who do not know that they do wrong* (5:1). This means when you come to God, you need to proceed with caution. When you are confused and angry, it makes sense that you want answers to your questions. But here's the thing: the person who speaks first, whether it's a question or an accusation, sets the agenda for the conversation. If you aren't careful, you can put yourself in God's rightful place. But as you saw in His response to Job, God's the One who should be asking the questions. You need to listen and listen well.

Don't approach God in worship so He can hear you better. Approach Him so you can hear *Him* better. He's got a perspective you don't. He sees further along the horizon than you do. You don't even know if you're asking the right questions. He knows, even if you don't.

When you come to God in worship, as the Teacher says, *Do not be quick with your mouth, do not be hasty in your heart to utter anything before God* (5:2). If you've got

chapter four

55

JOHN ONWUCHEKWA

Approach
God so you
can hear Him
better. He's got
a perspective
you don't.

Approach

you

Him

s got

ctive

you don't

something to say, keep it short and to the point. Be patient, as God is patient with you. Worship is about trusting God, even in the silence, and believing that in all things God works for the good of those who trust in Him (Romans 8:28).

And as you worship, prepare for celebration. When God speaks, good things happen. His words create light in the darkness (Genesis 1), cause paraplegics to give standing ovations (Acts 3), and bring the dead to life (John 11). It's safe to say your words, as good as they are, don't have that kind of power. Receive the joy, comfort, and peace that come when you realize you probably just need to talk less and listen more. Open your ears. God is already speaking.

Come Together

Pray with me.

Father,
        My loving Creator, I trust You. Speak,
for I am listening.
                        Amen.

Ecclesiastes concludes with the following passage:

Now all has been heard;
here is the conclusion of the matter:
Fear God and keep his commandments,
for this is the duty of all mankind.
For God will bring every deed into judgment,
including every hidden thing,
whether it is good or evil.

Ecclesiastes 12:13-14

You might bristle at being told you're going to be held accountable for how you live, but that's actually good news. It means God cares about your life. It is *meaningful* to Him. It matters. Now you can go on living with purpose, knowing that your life will actually count for something. But you still need an action plan. And thankfully, you don't have to figure it out all by yourself. You've got me, you've got the Teacher, and most importantly, you've got God—your Creator.

Over the rest of our time together, we are going to have a conversation about the things we spend so much of our lives chasing after—hoping, even praying, they'll fulfill us. So, yeah, knowledge, pleasure, money, work, and justice are coming up next. Then we'll talk about the adversity we face along the way. And last but by no means least, we'll explore what it means to live this life together, finding purpose in the joys and sorrows, even in the face of death.

With much wisdom

comes much sorrow;

the more knowledge,

the more grief.

ECCLESIASTES 1:18

chapter five

the miseducation of
john onwuchekwa

It's the middle of summer 2016. Westside Atlanta. I'm impatiently waiting at Popeyes for my two piece and a biscuit. The usual. Me and the cashiers are exchanging the kind of pleasantries that come when you know someone's face but not their name. Friendly and familiar. A year and half earlier, Shawndra and I bought a house out here. It's an investment property, but not in the way you might think. We hoped to see things change in this area of town, and we figured that families planting roots here would be a good idea. Our home is our way of *investing* in the community. 'Cause it's one thing to peer at the brokenness of this world through the blinds of a nice neighborhood's safety and seclusion. It's another thing entirely to make your home in the middle of the place you hope to change. A lot of people don't have the choice (that's what poverty does; it robs you of choices). But we did. We wanted to be part of the solution and *thought* we knew how to help. And sure enough, back in that Popeyes line, I get a chance to help.

As soon as I pull out my wallet to pay, a man comes up and asks me for money. You know the type. His body's the only suitcase he owns, so he's wearing too many clothes for the summer heat. I'm not quite sure how old he is, but I'm certain he doesn't wear his age well. I'm determined to help, but I ain't the one to feed his addiction. I ain't gonna be hustled like that. I'm gonna feed the man.

Let me buy you some food, I say. *Whatever you want.*

He orders twelve dollars' worth. More than my meal, but that's cool. I know I won't miss the money. I give him the claim check and take my seat, and the corners of my mouth start to curl toward the ceiling. I'm low-key feeling good about myself. I have used my knowledge and my experience. I knew what to do, and I did it. *Changing this community is going to be easier than I imagined.* Or so I think. As soon as I give him the claim check, I see him approaching some dude at a table on the other side of the restaurant. He strikes up a conversation and trades three crumpled dollar bills for the claim check. *My* claim check! Before I can protest, he's out the door (dang, he's fast for an old dude).

Now I'm beyond mad. I make my way over to confront the guy at the table. *What you doin', man? You know that ain't right.*

I expect to see him sink in shame, but I'm hit by a wave of rebuke.

Man, I've got five kids at home that need feedin', and my job don't pay enough. I've gotta take care of my kids.

Reality hits home as my self-righteousness is exposed. Here's a father hustling for his kids. He could be doing a whole lot of worse things to make ends meet. Instead, he trades a few dollars to keep his family fed. The cashier calls my number. I get my food and make my exit, avoiding eye contact with everyone. All I can think of is my inadequacy and a father's desperation. Like the Teacher says, *The more knowledge, the more grief* (1:18).

It turns out I didn't know nearly as much as I thought. And eventually, the more I learned about what the people in my community *really* needed, the more troubled I became. I began to lament.

Breathe

A little knowledge can be a dangerous thing, even (or especially) when you're trying to help someone. I thought I was doing the right thing, and maybe I got halfway there in the end, but I still had much to learn about how to truly help my neighbors.

Here's the thing: we may never know the whole story and all the struggles of the people around us. That's okay; God does. The next time you see an opportunity to help someone, pray that God would give you guidance. He knows and loves the person you're trying to help even more than you do. And here's even better news: God knows and loves you too. He'll take whatever you offer the person you're trying to help and multiply it.

FROM LEARNING TO LAMENT

For y'all optimists out there, I understand if you're resistant to the idea that learning leads to lament. Y'all think more knowledge will be the solution to whatever problem you're facing. Maybe it's personal, social, or even global. And, yeah, knowledge *can* help. It can help you accomplish amazing things. But it's not going to give you the relief that you seek.

Here's what I mean. Years back I went with a team to Guatemala to dig freshwater wells. We'd use this big machine and go deep into the ground. But no matter what, no matter how long it took, we would always find the water. Always. And with that water came refreshment.

Maybe you think knowledge is like that. Maybe I did too. Dig deep enough into problems, and eventually you'll find a solution. But it doesn't work that way. Knowledge is more like digging deep only to find you're in a bottomless pit. There's no refreshment to be found. There's nothing to quench your thirst.

I slouched out of Popeyes, got in my car, and headed home. I went to "The Shed." (Remember The Shed? It's my study in the backyard.) When we bought the house, I paid some friends to fix it up. It had been a workshop with tools on the walls. When you needed something fixed up, you'd take it in there. Now it's much different. Much nicer. Books have replaced the tools. Now I go to The Shed to put my thoughts together.

I want to know more, so I start reading. I look up references. I order books. I begin to dig deep, trying to learn about everything that happened earlier in the day. An addict wearing his wardrobe in the summer heat; a father struggling to feed his kids; a relatively well-to-do pastor who had every intention of helping, but was left feeling helpless. Did I find relief? Nah. I dug for water, but all I found was a bottomless pit.

> Experience told me that people treated me differently because of the color of my skin.

I learned about systemic poverty, the racial wealth gap, redlining, and a history of the government bailing out banks, so long as they weren't Black-owned. The situation at Popeyes was a symptom of a deeper sickness in my nation. Experience had already told me that even as the son of Nigerian immigrants, America looked at and treated me differently because of the color of my skin. I just didn't know how deep it went. *Learning led me to lament.*

A STEP IN THE RIGHT DIRECTION

The Teacher says, *Of making many books there is no end, and much study wearies the body* (12:12). Now, you might read this and think, *You know what? I don't need to know. I've got enough troubles of my own. I ain't got time for anyone else's, let alone what I can't control.* I feel you. But put yourself in another man's or woman's shoes.

What if you're the addict? What if you're the father? What if you're the pastor trying to help?

Let me challenge you. When you look at the world, what troubles you most? Pick up a book and read about it. Cover to cover. But don't stop there. Take one reference from the back of that book and follow it up. Don't expect to be refreshed, but at least you know you're taking a step in the right direction.

TRANSFORM KNOWLEDGE
INTO PURPOSE

Now, here's another thing to consider. Sometimes knowledge, if pursued for the wrong reasons, can release you from personal responsibility. It can justify your inaction. This snuck up on me in seminary. I had given myself to learning the Bible. Yet I found that the deeper I dove into

Learn more about what troubles you so you
can move in the direction of changing it.

the truths of Scripture and my own heart, the more I used my learning to bypass Scripture's implications for my life. God was convicting me about some things, and I didn't want to hear it. Yeah, I was digging, but I wasn't really looking for water. I was looking for an exit.

This is nothing new. Most people know Jesus' parable of the good Samaritan (Luke 10:25–37). What people don't remember, though, is *why* He told the parable in the first place. Jesus was responding to an expert in the law who had asked Him, *Who is my neighbor?* (v. 29). Seems innocent enough. But think about it. An expert in the law who doesn't know his neighbor is like a doctor who doesn't know her patient. Something else is going on. This law expert was looking for a way out. He didn't want to be *everyone's* neighbor. All that expertise had only helped him sidestep one of God's greatest commandments—*"Love your neighbor as yourself"* (v. 27). He was no different than the "good church-goin' folk" in the parable who sidestepped one of their own, lying half-dead on the road.

Learning leads to lament. Knowledge, if pursued for the wrong reasons, can lead to self-deception. Does that mean you should leave it all behind? Not at all. Knowledge is one of God's many gifts to us. It should be pursued. But you need to put it in its rightful place. You need to make it serve its rightful purpose. And this means directing your pursuit from a knowledge of *something* to a knowledge of

Someone. If you want your knowledge to be purposeful, it must be *personal.*

Here's what I mean. Let me introduce you to my guy Digger. We share the same birthday. I took Dee out to lunch once at Little Five Points in Atlanta. He's homeless, but he hasn't always been that way. He used to be an engineer at GM. Then his wife and son died in a car crash, and everything just fell apart. Dee went into a deep depression. Lost his job. Lost his house. This wasn't someone without knowledge. His knowledge just couldn't save him. He needed people to know him, to love him, to be with him as his life spiraled out of control. And this is true of so many on the streets. They aren't stupid. In fact, many, like Dee, are very smart. It's just that what they know doesn't count for much. They need relationships, support networks, and social opportunities.

I asked Dee what frustrates him most about the people who walk by him every day at Little Five Points. I expected to hear him complain about how they ignore a fellow human who is reaching out to them in need. Nope. He said his biggest frustration is seeing these people walk back and forth with no idea they depend upon God *for everything.* They just don't *know.*

> *Knowing* God is different from knowing *about* God.

Dee helped me see so clearly. If you want your search for knowledge to draw water, if you want to get out of that bottomless pit, you need to get to the source. You need to know God.

Fam, it's one thing to know *about* God. It's another thing—as the late, great J. I. Packer said—to *know* God. Don't get the two confused. Treat God like He's something to know about, and you'll end up no better than the expert in the law, looking for loopholes instead of loving his neighbor. But actually *knowing* God? To know the One who knows you better than you know yourself? To know the One who actually understands the causes of brokenness in our lives and in our world and has the power to heal them? That's the kind of personal knowledge you need.

Breathe

Dig deep in your own strength, with all your limitations and blind spots, and you'll find you're in nothing but a bottomless pit. Turn to God, and your lament will find lasting purpose and refreshment in times of need.

Jesus said, *"Let anyone who is thirsty come to me and drink. Whoever believes in me, as Scripture has said, rivers of living water will*

TRUST THE ONE WHO
KNOWS EVERYTHING

Our thirst for knowledge needs to be a pursuit for the type of knowledge that leads to joy. The ancient prophet Jeremiah is a case in point. He knew God. And God knew him: *"Before I formed you in the womb,"* He said to Jeremiah, *"I knew you"* (Jeremiah 1:5). God told Jeremiah, *"Let not the wise boast of their wisdom or the strong boast of their strength. . . . But let the one who boasts boast about this: that they have the understanding to know me"* (9:23–24). Our pursuit for God leads to a knowledge—a knowing—that brings joy.

What happens when your knowledge of yourself and your surroundings drives you to despair? You don't have to flounder in despondency. When you turn to God, your lament will find lasting purpose. Knowing God gives purpose to your daily life when there seem to be no apparent solutions to your daily problems. Let the feeling of dependence cause you, and encourage you, to cry out to Him anytime for anything. The more you put your eyes on God and take your eyes off yourself and your surroundings, the more you are willing to put your concerns and heartache on the One who exists beyond the sun. He's the answer to your agony.

Father,

> *I want to know You more. The problems of this world seem unending, but they are nothing compared to the hope I have in You. Teach me Your ways. Grant me Your wisdom. Refresh me through Your Spirit. May I be a source of living water to those living in lament.*
>
> *Amen.*

I denied myself

nothing my

eyes desired;

I refused my heart

no pleasure.

ECCLESIASTES 2:10

can't get enough

Pleasure. Maybe not the first thing that comes to mind after the pursuit of knowledge. But if you really think about it, they're closely related.

Take college, for example. It's known for two things, right? Studying and partying. One feeds the other. The head gets filled and filled, then the body says: *Hold up—it's my turn now.* Part of it is just giving your head a break. And another part of it illustrates the truth we talked about last chapter: knowledge doesn't truly satisfy. We crave something else to fill the void, and pleasure is the natural drug of choice. But that doesn't satisfy either. The Teacher had the same experience. He pursued pleasure because knowledge didn't get him where he wanted to go. He gave himself to entertainment—laughter, wine, gardens, servants, riches, and women—but just as he did with knowledge, he found he was still just chasing after the wind.

While many of us might take that path, even more pursue pleasure to distract us from our troubles. It offers a welcome amnesia. J. Cole raps about this in "Lights Please." It's a song about sex, but not in the way you'd expect. He's talking to his lady friend about all of life's brokenness, and how life in this country feels like an uphill stream for people who look like them. But all she wants to do is have sex, and he's more than happy to oblige. He finds the burden of knowledge too heavy, the attraction of relief too great. Like J. Cole, when we come up against the problems of the world and realize our powerlessness to change them, pleasure can provide much-needed relief. But the high doesn't last, and the problems haven't left.

Maybe you're reading this and you're thinking: *John, is this going to be just another sermon about how pleasure is bad and how I need to feel guilty about enjoying myself?* Not at all. In fact, the opposite is true. Pleasure is good. Really good. More than that, it's a gift from God. Your trouble isn't that you're pursuing pleasure; it's that you're setting your sights too low. You treat it like a main course when it's really a taste of what's to come.

One of the biggest obstacles preventing us from understanding pleasure's true purpose is our fixation on *morality*. We ask, is the pleasure good or bad? Now, I'm not saying morality isn't important; I'm telling you that the difference isn't as important as paying attention to the misguided belief that pleasure will truly satisfy. As Christians, sometimes we spend so much time obsessing over guilt and shame that we never really consider, *Is what I'm after really fulfilling?* How often has the pursuit of pleasure only led to addiction, isolation, and brokenness? And I don't mean just the immoral stuff, like illicit drugs and illegal activities. It could be innocent—a new car, another house. Or it could be a new partner, the high you get from your phone buzzing about another like on Instagram. Right or wrong, it still leaves us empty, craving more.

DIGGING BEHIND "NEVER ENOUGH"

I wish you could meet Harlie. She knows what's up. I met her over a decade ago at the bakery next door to my church in downtown Atlanta. I'd go there five days a week and order coffee. You want to get better at turning strangers into friends? Here's a pro tip: *Remember names.* Someone's first name is the sweetest word in any language. Sounds simple, right? But I've found that if you ask someone's name and then make sure you call them by their name, about the third time they start feeling insecure about not knowing yours. And so the questions begin. Before you know it, meaningless interactions—like me ordering the same cup of coffee every day—transform into meaningful relationships. And that's what happened with Harlie.

Come Together

You feeling disconnected? Maybe you find yourself seeing the same people over and over but never actually getting to know them. Let me help you out.

- Write down a couple of the places you frequent. Maybe, like me, it's a place where you get coffee.
- Leave a space for the names of the folks you interact with but otherwise don't know.
- Here's my challenge—see if you can fill that

> space with a name. Maybe you'll find that
> by the third time you mention their name,
> you've got a lot more to write about the
> relationship you've started to build.

Harlie and I got to talking. Her story read like an after-school special. She gave her life to drugs too young. And as anyone knows who's experienced that firsthand, or is close to someone who has, the drugs are never enough. But thank God Harlie's rock bottom was an awakening, not an early grave. God gave her the gift of desperation. She left the drugs behind and started running instead. And I mean, *twenty-six point two miles* in the Atlanta sun running! She loved it—the thrill, the accomplishment. The steady drumbeat of hands clapping as she neared the finish line was her favorite song. Or it was, until she realized that running had become just another drug, another kind of addiction. It wasn't immoral. But it proved every bit as destructive. Just like before, her whole life was consumed by the pursuit.

Fam, I was shocked. I had thought the problem was what Harlie was chasing. Running is a whole lot healthier than cocaine, right? *John,* she said, *I found that when I made running the center of my life, there wasn't enough of that either.* It wasn't the drugs or the running; it was the

> Realizing she had more
> than she needed and
> still wasn't satisfied
> awakened her.

addictive pursuit of something that could never satisfy. What she did wasn't nearly as important as *why* she did it. That's left a lasting impression on me.

Years after that interaction with Harlie, I read Judith Grisel's book *Never Enough*. Judith's pursuit started at thirteen years old with a bottle of wine. It put a straitjacket on her out-of-control nerves and anxieties. *So, this is how people get through life*, she thought. She then went on to try every kind of drug until the age of twenty-three, when she got clean. Unlike Harlie, though, she didn't bottom out. More like the Teacher, she found herself on the mountaintop, with more drugs than she could ever want. But that turned out to be her awakening. *I have more than I could possibly need, and it's still not enough.* Amazingly, she went back to school and got a PhD in neuroscience. She wanted to understand the relationship between the human brain and addictive behaviors. And here's what she found: We don't become addicts because our brains are broken, but because they are working properly. We are designed to always want more.

> We are designed
> to want more.

Think about that. Your brain will get used to the most intense pleasures only to crave *more*. See what I'm saying?

The fundamental issue isn't whether pleasure is good or bad; it's that there is something deep inside of you that pleasure can never fill. From lines of cocaine to the finish lines of marathons, it can all end up being the same pursuit. The destination is always out of reach.

Breathe

What pleasure do you lean on when you're stressed and anxious? What pursuit is at the center of your day? Is there something that makes you think, *If only I had just a little more of that, I'd feel alright?*

Y'all, I don't want you to feel guilty or ashamed. It's just me and you talking; you don't have to tell anyone else. But like Harlie and Judith, maybe it's time for a revelation.

Does your need for pleasure hide a deeper longing?

Let's pray.

Father,

Thank You for Your love for me. May Your Spirit awaken me. I want to stop

> *chasing the things that won't ever satisfy.*
> *I want to run to You. Thanks for remind-*
> *ing me Your arms are open wide.*
>
> *Amen.*

WHAT'S YOUR PLEASURE?

Judith didn't know it, but her studies in neurology only confirmed what C. S. Lewis had observed years before in his book *Mere Christianity*: If we find ourselves with a desire that nothing in this world can satisfy, the most probable explanation is that we were made for another world.[1]

You know this is true. Don't you feel a deep longing for something more? When you're soaring on the highest pleasures—don't you wish they'd never end? Sex is a case in point. Who wants *that* to end? At its best, sex is a physical, emotional, and spiritual union. It offers euphoria, intimacy, acceptance, and belonging. It puts a Do Not Disturb sign on the door to your heart—so anxiety knows it isn't welcome. It also provides a welcome amnesia that J. Cole raps about. You're aren't thinking about the bills that need to be paid or the meeting coming up. You're lost in the fullness of that joyful present. But here's the thing, y'all: it always comes to an end. Part of being in a broken world means there's always a separation. Bitterness mixes with the sweet. Selfishness creeps between the sheets. An argument waits patiently in the next room. A temptation might be tapping you on the shoulder, whispering, *There's someone else.*

But what if there's more to it than that? What if sex isn't just an end in itself? What if it's a promise, a foretaste of something else? What if our unending desire for an unceasing intimacy and euphoria isn't misplaced, but actually points to a deeper reality about who we really are, about who *you* really are? What if it's saying, *You are made for eternity?*

THERE'S PURPOSE IN PLEASURE

Hold up, though. Maybe you think pleasure and God are like oil and water. You've been told to feel guilty about those longings and desires. You've been told God wants you to draw a line in the sand between the good and bad kinds of pleasure. Fam, I think you need to come to Jesus.

When you do, here's what you'll find: Jesus' first miracle takes place at a wedding. Look it up; it's in the Gospel of John. He turns the equivalent of hot dog water into Napa Valley's finest. And what's the last thing Jesus does with His disciples before He lays down His life? He doesn't feed them a prison meal of bread and water. Nah. He has a Passover Feast with his friends. Lots of wine there. And what does He say is waiting for us when this life is done? Another feast! One that won't end! So, you can think what you want about pleasure and God not mixing; just don't say it comes from the Bible.

God gave you your eternal appetite. You have been made to experience pleasure in all its fullness. But like so many things, you can turn that gift into a curse if you put it to the wrong purpose. Pleasure isn't supposed to make you grasp ever more tightly to your passing life. It is meant to loosen your grip on life and point you to God, to make you long for the eternal pleasures of heaven, which will one day make their way to earth (Revelation 21). And even though pleasure can help alleviate life's pain, that's not its true purpose. The purpose of pleasure is to be a pathway to God, the Giver of that pleasure. Otherwise it ultimately brings you to the same place as Harlie and Judith, or worse. Whether there isn't enough or too much, you'll still be wanting more—and killing yourself to get it.

So, where do you go now? Don't cast your eyes down in despair. Set your sights higher.

My friend Nancy taught me this. She's an old lady who used to go to our church. One day she asked me to go for a walk. I hate the outside, but I love Nancy, so I obliged. As we were walking and I was talking, she interrupted me with the firmness and politeness that only older ladies can. *John,* she said, *look at those trees.*

The purpose of pleasure is to be a pathway
to God, the Giver of that pleasure.

I didn't see what she saw. I mean, I saw trees—but what's the big deal?

She kept going. *Isn't God so good that He gave us those colors to look at?*

We were looking in the same place, but I didn't see half of what she saw. There was pleasure there that I couldn't enjoy because my eyes weren't as prepared to appreciate it. Nancy traced every pleasure to its Giver. Her enjoyment of the colors led her to the enjoyment of God. Her eternal palate got a taste of eternal pleasure, and she was satisfied. If pleasure becomes your end, there's never enough. But if you see it as a pathway, you'll find there's more of it than you could possibly enjoy in a thousand lifetimes.

What's Your Story?

Tell me, what do you enjoy? What are your "colors in the trees"? Next time you're at it, give yourself pause. *What does this enjoyment tell me about how I'm made? What does it tell me about my Maker?*

Pleasure is a foretaste of a greater fulfillment waiting for you beyond the grave. With age, your senses may fade, but your desire won't. Just ask Nancy.

Try this one on for size. Next time you sit down for a meal, forgo the prayer at the beginning of the meal and save it for the end. Why? So you can say "thank You" for the food you have *enjoyed*. It'll remind you, as it reminds us, that pleasure is a gift. God didn't have to make this food taste so good. He didn't have to give us the senses to appreciate it. But the gift needs to lead us to the Giver. And that's the purpose of pleasure.

Father,

Give me eyes to see what folks like Nancy see so well. Expand my palate so I can better appreciate all You've given me to enjoy. But don't let me get so fixated on these pleasures that I lose sight of You. Make them transparent. Help me look through them to gain a clearer vision of You—the One who turns hot dog water to wine, the Giver of pleasures that will never end.

Amen.

Whoever loves money

never has enough;

whoever loves wealth is

never satisfied with

their income.

This too is meaningless.

ECCLESIASTES 5:10

chapter seven

run the jewels

Money can't buy happiness. I know. You know. We all know. It doesn't stop us from trying, though. Why? Because money has that *glow*. It's like your favorite model all oiled up on the glossy cover of a magazine. You know what I'm saying—curves and muscles in all the right places, hair just right, no wrinkles in sight. It says, *I'm your dream come true.* We know they've been airbrushed. We know they've been trimmed. But we like to believe they always look this good. And that's the way we see money, isn't it? We don't think of the stress and the sacrifice. We don't consider the people who get stepped on or stepped over just so others can accumulate more. We're committed to seeing money in its best light, even if the light is artificial. Why? Because that's what you do when you're in love. And when it comes to money, we're in love.

All right, y'all. It's time to take out the makeup wipes and take off the waist trainer. Let that gut out and turn the filter off. I'm going to show you what money really looks like before it's touched up. My tools for the task: a bank error, Leo Tolstoy, and a little Nigerian generosity from my folks. And when we're done, I'm going to make sure you got a hold on your money so your money ain't got a hold on you.

ALL THAT POWER

Money. We overestimate its ability to satisfy and underestimate its ability to sour. And I should've known all that just by listening to the Teacher:

> If you see the poor oppressed in a district, and justice and
>   rights denied, do not be surprised at such things. . . .
> Whoever loves money never has enough;
> whoever loves wealth is never satisfied with their income.
>
> **Ecclesiastes 5:8, 10**

But I guess I couldn't take his word for it. The glow was too enticing, the magazine cover too appealing. I had to go ahead and learn it for myself. I was playing hard to get with wisdom. Thank God she's relentless.

It's 2009, and Shawndra and I are ready to move to Atlanta during an economic downturn. Shawn got us set. *Let's save up all our sick days and then cash out before we move.* Fast-forward, we're about to leave, and it's payday. I check our account. There's a smudge on the screen I can't seem to rub off. Wait a minute, that smudge is a . . . *comma*? Listen, back then I was used to seeing commas in sentences, never in bank statements. And the number was staring at me, inviting me to daydream about all the things I could do with it.

I waved Shawn over. We didn't say a word because we didn't have to. Our smiles were subtitled, *All our problems are solved.* A great weight came off our shoulders. If contentment is a balloon, then that money was our helium. We were sky high.

What's Your Story?

Has money ever had an effect on you? It probably depends a lot on your background. What were the messages you received about money when you were growing up?

- If you grew up poor, how many of your
  problems were blamed on a lack of money?
- If you grew up rich, how often were problems
  solved by throwing money at them?
- If you grew up middle class, how much of your life
  did you spend envying someone else's ability to
  spend? Or maybe you experienced just enough
  of money's benefits, without experiencing the
  pitfalls that come with its excess.

Regardless of where you're from, though, how
have these messages about money shaped your life?
How have they impacted your spending habits?

Understand, I'm not trying to condemn money.
It can do a lot of good in the right hands and for
the right purposes. You just need to see it clearly
for what it is. You need to take off the makeup.

So, what happened to that balloon? It ran out of air real
quick. The bank recognized the clerical error in a couple
hours, and we went crashing back to the earth. Why did I
think all my problems were solved? Where did the feeling
of instant relief, joy, and satisfaction come from?

If I'm really going to come clean? The love of money.

'Cause when you love someone or something, you *want* to see it in its best light, right? Well, that was me. I bought the lie.

I don't need to tell you that the love of money corrupts. But we too easily convince ourselves that it just corrupts *other* people. Let me let you in on something. You are "other people." It's dangerous for everybody. Greed and oppression are like middle school lovebirds with interlocking fingers; they're impossible to pull apart. Like Lester Freamon tells a rookie cop in *The Wire*: follow the drugs, and you'll get drug addicts and dealers; follow the money, and you don't know where it's going to take you. Slavery, sex trafficking, private prisons, political scandals—the list could go on forever. Just like the apostle Paul said, the love of money is at the root of them all (1 Timothy 6:10).

Why do you think this truth is so hard to accept? Sure, we know the love of money is dangerous and that it can't buy happiness, but what is it about money that still has us saying—like the hook in my friend Swoope's song—*Money can't buy happiness, but I wouldn't mind cryin' in a Lambo*? Maybe it's 'cause we've been thinking all we need is to get a hold of more money, when money's really had a hold on us this whole time.

Part of the reason greed has such power over us is that we don't really

We know money can't buy happiness because we don't really know how much money we need. There's no magic amount.

know how much money we need. There's no magic number. Leo Tolstoy illustrates the problem in his short story, "How Much Land Does a Man Need?" He writes about a peasant named Pahom, who is given the opportunity to take as much land as he wants in a single day. The catch is that he needs to draw the boundary marker himself, and the line needs to be completed before sundown. So he starts early. But his greed rises early too and comes along for the ride. Partway through he realizes he's tried to take too much and will lose it all if he can't make it back to the starting point in time. So he runs, and runs, and *just* makes it—only to drop dead from exhaustion. Pahom is buried in a six-foot plot of land. Turns out, that was all the land he *needed*. It's a sobering thought. But that's the Teacher's lesson. You can chase after money, but you'll never arrive at your destination. Why? Because in so many ways a life spent chasing money is a life turning its back on contentment.

> You can chase after money, but there's no real destination.

Breathe

Fam, there's a better way. You don't need to follow in Pahom's footsteps. There shouldn't be a number on your happiness. But let's suppose there is.

- Try and imagine the amount. Maybe someone is offering you the chance to pay off your debt forever. Maybe you've been given a blank check. How much do you need?
- Once you've got the amount, I want you to read Jesus' words to the rich young ruler in Matthew 19:21: *"If you want to be perfect, go, sell your possessions and give to the poor, and you will have treasure in heaven. Then come, follow me."*
- Put yourself in the ruler's place. Between the amount and Jesus' command, what would you choose? What's holding you back?

Let's pray.

Father,

You ask a lot. You ask me what I truly value in this world. And when I hear Your command to the rich young ruler, maybe I don't like the answer that emerges in my heart. Help me embrace Your offer without condition. I want to follow You.

Amen.

THE PRICE TAG ON HAPPINESS

Hear me out. The point isn't that money *itself* is evil. The problem is the *love* of money. And the difference between the two can be enormous. One gets you fed; the other feeds on you. You need to know where you stand. The last thing you want is to be that rich young ruler, who walked away from his Savior because the money was too enticing.

Money isn't evil. The problem with money is when people love it in a way that becomes destructive.

So, how do you know if you've fallen in love with money? Here's some of the usual symptoms.

If there's nothing else to think about, money
  immediately comes to mind.
You scheme to get more of it.
You dream of what you'll do with it.
An abundance of money fills you with joy and hope.
It's the answer to your problems.
The cost to your quality of life is significant, but
  you don't feel free to say *no* because the money's
  too good.
The value of money outweighs any other concern.

If you are experiencing any of these symptoms, money's probably got a hold on your heart.

I want you to have the freedom to say *no* to money. I want you to *enjoy* money without loving it. And I want you to know that it's not only possible—I've actually seen it with my own two eyes.

SLIPPING OUT FROM MONEY'S GRASP

I grew up in a pretty well-off family. My dad's a highly educated and successful entrepreneur and humanitarian. My mom's cut from the same cloth. She's got a doctorate in education and has worked in educational administration her whole life. But even though my parents could afford them, I never got new Jordans like the rest of the dudes I grew up with. In the early 2000s, I was rocking hand-me-downs that put me at the cutting edge of mid-90s fashion. Was it because my parents loved money? Just the opposite. They *loved* giving it away!

> My parents' wealth was seen in their giving.

I saw them give *tens* of thousands of dollars. They sent money back to Nigeria. They gave away cars. People lived with us off and on, and I never saw them pay a grocery bill or pick up their share of the utilities. My folks covered it all. And I didn't see nothing but smiles and contentment. Their wealth was in their giving. It was, and still is, deeply satisfying. My parents had money. Money didn't have them. And that's the difference. If you can't give it away freely, it's not because you don't have it. It's because it has you.

Let's Connect

If you are getting a sinking feeling right now, I'm the last person who's going to judge you. Remember the bank error? Money may have a hold on you, but it doesn't have to stay that way. Like any change in behavior, it's going to take a combination of factors—in this case, *practice* and *liberation*.

When talking about freedom from slavery, Frederick Douglass said, *I prayed for freedom for twenty years, but received no answer until I prayed with my legs.* If you need to be released from the love of money, absolutely *pray* for freedom. But make sure you also put that prayer into practice.

First things first. Let's pray.

> Father,
> Release me from the love of money.
> Free me so I can give freely to those in
> need. Show me how to use my money
> and resources to honor You.
>
> Amen.

Now, here's a couple of ways to put that prayer into practice:

1. Set a giving goal. Shawn and I have a monthly budget, and the first thing on the list is how much we're giving away that month. We do that before we account for anything else. That way we're giving our firstfruits to those in need and not the scraps from our table.

2. Get some cash in hand. Near our church there's always a few folks selling things like bottles of water on the corner. Thanks to an economy that increasingly depends on credit cards, it's become an ever-convenient excuse to say, *Sorry, brother, no cash.* Lose the excuse. Be intentional. Have cash ready in your car so you can say yes the next time. You can even ask for a name. On the third time,

maybe there's a relationship ready to get started, a door could be opening for someone's way out.

Money has the power to change relationships dramatically. Just ask those tragic few who win the lottery each year. They'll tell you how their friends and family began to see them as little more than a number. And that's just one example in a million—from a divorce over debt to another friendship ruined because, *It's not personal, it's just business*. But you can be part of the change. If you don't love money more than you love your neighbor, your money can set people *free*. My parents showed me how, and I try to follow in their steps. You can too.

The main lesson I learned from my parents is that contentment isn't just the result of hard work. You can't practice your way into contentment. We have to be transformed from the inside out. When Jesus talks about the dangers of the love of money, He uses an interesting metaphor: slaves and masters (Matthew 6:24). His point—money doesn't just want to be loved; it wants to be lord. Money wants to be the sun around which we orbit. That's the danger. It has this enslaving power.

The good news is that Jesus does a lot more than just give us

When viewed from the proper perspective, money has the ability to set people free, to help those in need.

good advice or principles to follow. He liberates us. His death and resurrection, complete with a promise of a new life full of treasures that can't be lost, remind us that there's a type of security money can't buy. There are riches of contentment, peace, and love that no currency can afford. This good news, these great gifts, are freely given to anyone who's willing to accept.

Through His life, we learn that contentment has nothing to do with a number. It has to do with freedom and salvation. It has to do with fullness of life—right now and in the life to come. Jesus can save you. Given the chance, money would rather enslave you. So, put your treasure in the right place. Ask yourself—*Where's my money?* Does it own property in your head and heart? Or do you hold it in the palm of an open hand? Freely received, freely given.

JOHN ONWUCHEKWA

What do people get for all the
toil and anxious striving with
which they labor under the
sun? All their days their work
is grief and pain; even at
night their minds do not rest.

ECCLESIASTES 2:22–23

unfinished business

It's April 5, 2021. Baylor's just shocked the world. I'm watching at the crib by myself instead of being front and center at half-court because we're still in a pandemic. But it's all good. I feel like I'm right there. That's my alma mater. Those are my guys. I feel part of that win. And as I watch them celebrate, it washes up a flood of memories. Y'all haven't forgotten about that stickup in Nigeria, right? Well, that changed the trajectory of my life. Instead of heading to Sam Houston State to walk-on and play basketball with my brother Sam, I rerouted and went to Baylor. I was going to try and follow in his footsteps, by walking-on at a different school. A bigger school.

ENJOY THE EFFORT,
RELEASE THE RESULTS

Like my dad, Sam was the *hardest* of workers. He graduated college in three years, then spent his fourth finishing up a master's degree while teaching the very classes some of his teammates were taking, investing in real estate, *and* playing on the team. He worked for his goals and got them. I was determined to be like that.

All right, go back with me a bit. It's 2003. After an unsuccessful attempt to walk-on my freshman year, I come back the next summer ready to try again when I hear the Baylor program has just been leveled. (Google it—one of the biggest scandals in college basketball history.) One player murdered another, the coach tried to cover it up—the script reads like a Lifetime movie, but it actually happened. The best players got to transfer, and that meant the team went from no walk-ons to having a few slots available. I was determined to slide in. But I never quite got there. So, for two years I'm in basketball purgatory—a practice player who exists as something between a walk-on and a manager. All the burdens, none of the benefits. And every day on the practice floor I try to catch a break. I dive for balls, take charges, and try to win every sprint, hoping to work my way out of purgatory. I put all that work in; it just doesn't work out. My senior year I quit the team.

> I could have spent more time enjoying the work.

That year I was so full of regret. Equally bitter and disappointed. All that time, all that work, and I hadn't accomplished a thing. That future I imagined never came. Years later, as I watch my guys on the floor, celebrating the program's entrance into the NCAA Promised Land after their wilderness wanderings, I reflect on how my perspective has changed. I've come to be grateful for those two hard years. I just wish that instead of working for a payoff that never came, I made the most of the moment. I wish I'd spent more time enjoying the work instead of stressing over an outcome.

What's Your Story?

Do you have regrets like that? Is there something that didn't go your way no matter how hard you tried? Fam, it's not just you. We all go through it, right? Let me help you out. Bring those regrets to mind. Maybe say them out loud. Just let them out.

Now let me bless you. Don't let that disappointment hang over you like a cloud. The past is in the past, but it still can be redeemed. Bring it to God. For all you know He still has plans to use everything you put in.

Father,

I give You my past failure and frustrations. If I have regrets, encourage me that it wasn't all for nothing. Remind me You're not finished writing my story. Only You know where that work will lead. And if I'm struggling now, help me trust that You'll honor my labor even if it doesn't lead to where I expect.

Amen.

THERE ARE NO GUARANTEES

Now, I've been talking about the way we work for some future payoff. But there's another, less appealing, way to say the same thing—we work 'cause we're *worried*. We're worried about the future and our place in it. The uncertainty keeps us up at night, and we don't want our lives to count for nothing. And if you're like me, you also worry about the next generation. I want Ava to have a secure future, filled with opportunity. What can I do to make that happen?

We believe work offers some kind of promise, some guarantee, about our future. The kind that says, *If you put the work in, everything will work out*. But work can't make that promise. It can't cash that check. The future isn't merit-based; it's more like a lottery. As the Teacher says,

> The race is not to the swift
> or the battle to the strong,
> not does food come to the wise
> or wealth to the brilliant
> or favor to the learned;
> but time and chance happen to them all.
>
> **Ecclesiastes 9:11**

Your work isn't as secure of an investment as you think. It's a gamble. And the one thing everyone learns in gambling is the house always wins. Even if you succeed, you'll meet the same end as everyone else. Death is the great leveler.

All your life's work is just that—your *life's* work. You can't take anything you build into the next life, and you can't ensure the building won't collapse once you leave. The Teacher hated his work for this very reason. He knew he wouldn't even be able to rest in peace, 'cause eventually someone was going to undo his work, squandering his legacy and dishonoring his memory. Imagine MLK watching *Love & Hip Hop*. Forget spinning in his grave. He'd be tumbling in ways Simone Biles couldn't.

You can build a life now that will mean something to those affected by your choices.

MORE JOY, LESS STRESS

Don't get me get wrong. I'm not telling you to give up or to stop working hard. Hard work is good for the soul and necessary for you to reach your goals. Keep it going. But if your drive to work hard is fueled primarily by worry, you're going to run out of gas. Worry burns

Make sure your drive to work hard isn't fueled by worry.

quickly and burns you out even faster than work does. I want you to enjoy the present and to find meaning in your work.

Breathe

Try this threefold approach:

1. Work well now. The Teacher says, *Whatever your hand finds to do, do it with all your might, for in the realm of the dead, where you are going, there is neither working nor planning nor knowledge nor wisdom* (9:10). Find enjoyment in working to the best of your ability right now. No matter what it is, the more of yourself you invest, the more valuable it will

become to you. Don't stress over the outcome. A time is coming when all your work will cease.

2. Look to the future, but don't stare. Living in the present doesn't mean ignoring what's ahead. It's good to have goals. It's good to have plans. Just don't be so transfixed by what might or might not happen that you never get started on the work in front of you.

3. Let mystery fuel your work. Don't worry about the future. See opportunity in possibility. You don't know what's going to happen, so receive that as freedom to be creative. The Teacher knows: *Sow your seed in the morning, and at evening let your hands not be idle, for you do not know which will succeed* (11:6). Yours is the business of working. God's is the business of results.

Is this approach going to bring you success down the line? I don't know. And that's the thing. You don't either. But it will help give your work purpose. It will unchain your work from anxiety. It will help give you the freedom to enjoy the present. It may even open up your future in ways you never could have imagined—like what happened to me at Portrait Coffee.

A PORTRAIT OF PURPOSEFUL WORK

Y'all know Shaq once turned down a chance to get in early on a gang of Starbucks franchises, right? His reasoning— *Black folks don't drink coffee!* He laughs about it now, but he wasn't exactly wrong. You don't find a lot of specialty coffee shops in the hood. And that's no accident; there's a little backstory. Listen up.

When I first moved to Atlanta, I parked my car and rode the train system wherever it took me to try and learn the city. Here's what I noticed. You ride the train from South Atlanta to North and two things change: what's inside and what's outside. Inside, the color of the passengers goes from

Black and brown to white. Outside, the economic conditions of the city noticeably improve the further north you go. Basically, Black and brown folks take their exit before they reap the economic benefits of the city they helped build.

If you overlay the coffee supply chain with Atlanta's train system, the same thing happens. Coffee grows where Black and brown folks live—places like Ethiopia. They own and work the land that produces the second-most-consumed beverage in the world. They are the backbone of a $250 billion industry. Yet by the time you buy that eighteen-dollar bag in a coffee shop, Black and brown folks have already taken their exit.

My train ride to nowhere gave me a purpose and direction I never could have anticipated. My friends and I decided to open a coffee shop in the historic West End district. We called it Portrait because we wanted to change the picture that comes to mind when people think of specialty coffee. We also wanted to remind people that the color of their coffee is the same color as the skin of its inventors and producers—no matter how often the final product's been whitewashed.

Our main idea was the shop. Roasting our own coffee was just a good side hustle. We'd cut our cost of goods in half and make better margins. We raised $150,000 and signed a five-year lease on March 1, 2020. We had a plan, and all we had to do was work it. What could possibly go wrong? COVID-19. March 11, the NBA shuts down. March 12—the world.

The old me would've been deflated. He would've searched for

creative ways to give up but not lose face. All that work. *For what?* But I'd learned by then. I'd listened to the Teacher and taken his words to heart. We shifted and started slinging beans online. And then George Floyd was murdered, and the world got turned over again. Only this time it sparked interest and support in Black-owned businesses. There was a chance meeting with the COO of a $5 billion corporation, and then a spot on *Good Morning America*. And now, business is *nothing* like we expected, but so much more than we ever imagined.

As far as we knew, all our hard work was going to come to nothing. I may as well have been back on the Baylor practice courts, always hitting the floor, never rising above the ranks of a practice player. But we never really worried. We were too busy enjoying our work *in the moment*. We kept an eye on the future without losing perspective. We let mystery lead and gave ourselves the freedom to be creative. Now the seeds sown in our community have blossomed something crazy. Shaq would be proud. (If you happen to be in conversation with him and

The seeds
we've sown are
blossoming.

hear about him wanting to invest in another coffee franchise, tell him to hit me up.)

I struggled with whether to share this story with you. I don't want this to feel like a rags-to-riches story. (And trust me, I ain't rich.) I don't want you to come away from this thinking, *If I only work harder, if I just follow these steps, this will happen to me too.* 'Cause here's the deal: the same guy who worked to make the team is the guy who worked to roast the coffee. I couldn't control either outcome. The future's in God's hands, not mine. And the same is true for you.

TRUST GOD WITH YOUR WORK

During the Sermon on the Mount, Jesus looks at the people gathered around and basically tells them, *Don't worry. Don't worry about your life. Don't worry about your body. Don't worry about your food or clothes.* He tells them that their heavenly Father knows what they need and, if they seek Him first, He will provide. *Do not worry about tomorrow, for tomorrow will worry about itself. Each day has enough trouble of its own* (Matthew 6:34). Sometimes I wonder whether we've really taken these words to heart, especially when it comes to our work. Maybe we hear them as great advice, or even just a nice suggestion we can take or leave. But what if this is a command? *Do not worry.*

Are you still going to work entirely for the future, anxious about what it will bring? Troubles are coming regardless. The only guarantee we have in life is that *nothing* will be *everything* we hoped for. So, trust God with your work. The Teacher says our satisfaction is a gift from God, so receive it gladly (Ecclesiastes 3:13). Don't waste another day grasping for things you'll never hold—like the results of your work. Be free. Let mystery inspire your creativity. Plant those seeds in the morning and the evening. Who knows what the harvest may bring? Maybe coffee will grow in the opportunity desert that's your community. Only God knows. And you can take joy in that—discovering your purpose and enjoying your work.

Let's pray.

Father,

Take my work. It's Yours. Do with it what You will. When I find it hard, when it seems meaningless, when I'm not seeing the results I expect, remind me of Your faithfulness. You won't let it go to waste. And if my work reaps rewards, bring me back to praise You first for Your abundant generosity.

Free me from worry. Fill me with Your Spirit. My future is Yours, and I don't need to worry, 'cause it's in Your hands.

Amen.

I saw something else under the sun:

In the place of judgment—

wickedness was there,

in the place of justice—wickedness

was there.

I said to myself:

"God will bring into judgment

both the righteous and the wicked,

for there will be a time for every

activity,

a time to judge every deed."

ECCLESIASTES 3:16-17

one day it'll make sense

God is in control. God is just. God is good, all the time. And all the time, God is good.

I believe those statements with my whole heart. Then it happens again. Another video. There's another shooting. Another politicized court case. And like a bad movie, the beginning drama eventually fades into an anticlimactic ending. Few indictments. Renewed fears.

But my sadness refuses to be stained with teardrops anymore. They stopped a long time ago.

There's a pain that hurts so bad, it makes it difficult to *stop* crying. Most of us are accustomed to that. There's a type of pain that hurts so *deep* that sometimes it makes it impossible to *start* crying. I've been there for the last several years. With each video, I find myself heartbroken, but not surprised. My heart isn't newly broken each time (I haven't

119

fully put the pieces together since Trayvon). Each instance reminds me that my heart is still fractured.

Injustice rules our world. It's been that way for a very long time. The Teacher saw it too:

> Again I looked and saw all the oppression that was
> taking place under the sun:
> I saw the tears of the oppressed—
> and they have no comforter;
> power was on the side of their oppressors—
> and they have no comforter.
>
> **Ecclesiastes 4:1**

It's enough to make you give up, to doubt you could ever make a difference. God says He's in control, *but is He really?*

I've got news for you. Good news. He is!

The Teacher says, *God* will *bring into judgment both the righteous and the wicked* (3:17). His justice *will* be done. This future vision can fill you with hope to keep going. So, let's take an honest look at the world. Like the Teacher, let's keep it candid—'cause if we're blindsided by injustice, we're going to be blindfolded to hope. And we *need* the encouragement and inspiration that's only found in God's promise for the future. Justice is God's work, and He won't let it fail. He's got you!

GOD'S GOT YOU

I got you. Growing up, those three words were enough to make you float. Back in the day, if you didn't have a ride or enough cash and your homie said, *I got you*, you knew you were taken care of. You were straight. Well, that's the idea. Sometimes it doesn't work out that way.

Like my prom night. I brought LeKendra, my date, to an expensive steakhouse. I really wanted to impress her. So, when we took a look at the menu, I told her, *anything you want.*

Really?

I got you.

She ordered the salmon. There was no price, only something called *MKT rate*. Weird. But I wasn't sweating it. Well, not until the bill came. It was more money than I had in my bank account.

You okay, John?

Yeah, I got you.

I tried to say it confidently, but insecurity was dripping off my forehead and onto the check I couldn't pay. Her lips said, *Okay*, but I could tell she wasn't buying it. I swiped the card, and we left. Thankfully, the overdraft fees didn't kick in till the following Monday. I was shook regardless.

It's one of those stories that gets funnier the more the time passes. I promise you, though, it wasn't funny at the time. But it does illustrate the insecurity you feel when someone says, *I got you*, but you don't really believe them.

You believe God's *got you*, right? You believe that He's in control no matter what happens? But what do you do when someone causes you harm? They lie about you, mislead you, or betray you. They take advantage of you or someone you love. And then justice is delayed or even denied. You want to trust God through it all, but it's hard to understand what He's doing. Some might question God's goodness. Some might ask if God really cares. You just want to know why He hasn't taken care of you the way a Father should. You don't expect things to be painless or easy. You just want assurance that God's really *got you*.

Let's Connect

Are you in that place right now? You're crying out: *God, I believe—but I just don't see.* Don't give up. Keep seeking His face. Ask Him for a deeper awareness of His presence.

The earliest Christian monks in Egypt would memorize Psalm 70:1 to help them gain that awareness. It reminded them, too, that they shouldn't just seek God when they thought they needed Him, 'cause the truth is, they always needed Him. And not only that, He was always there, even if they weren't looking for Him. Same for us today.

So, let this psalm be your constant prayer:

> *Hasten, O God, to save me;*
> *come quickly, LORD, to help me.*
> *Amen.*

KEEP ON LOOKING

The need to believe God's *got me* comes up every time my social media timeline tells me the contrary. Lately, I've sat with the fact that *watching* murders isn't normal.

I know every generation has *heard* about them, but I've recently realized that there have been generations of people throughout history who never witnessed a murder caught on camera, and I've seen too many to count. I've seen so many, I don't even remember them all. Every time I see another senseless killing as I'm casually scrolling through my feeds, I ask: *God, have You got us?*

The feeling's compounded by the fact that we believe the American justice system is supposed to reflect, even if in a very limited way, God's justice. And yet, as the Teacher says, we find that even *in the place of justice—wickedness was there* (Ecclesiastes 3:16). Instead of providing security or care, the system habitually leaves us anxious, uncertain, even terrorized. We want to trust, but it's hard—sometimes, impossibly hard. I remember the horror of seeing my oldest brother, Emmanuel, sent to the hospital by a policeman who split open his left temple with a Maglite.

He fit the description of kids who'd gotten into a fight earlier that night. My brother still had his work uniform on. I remember my other brother, Sam, telling me how he was cuffed, thrown into the back of a cruiser, and taken to jail because of "warrants" an officer insisted belonged to him. The officer refused to check the name on my brother's license: Chinedum Chibuike Samuel Chukwunonso Onwuchekwa. There weren't a lot of folks with that name walking around Huntsville, Texas, in 2003.

I remember the chills sprinting down my spine and warm tears flooding my cheeks as I stared down the barrel of an officer's gun. At one point, the pistol was so close to my head I couldn't see it anymore. My crime? My friends and I were asking directions. We got lost downtown and were trying to get home. A strange sense of sadness and solidarity comes from realizing every Black man I've ever started this conversation with doesn't respond with the scripted sympathy you get from customer service agents: *I can't imagine how that makes you feel.*

Rather, every time I've started this conversation, it evolves into a tennis match where we volley these horror stories back and forth with smirks and smiles—not because they aren't uniquely horrible. They are. We don't cry anymore because the stories are unsurprisingly common. I remember how each of our stories ended the same way. We were reprimanded and lectured on how to avoid precarious situations like that one, and the men who caused our terror and trauma were free to go their way.

Until the summer of 2020, I couldn't tell these stories without some people thinking I was somehow to blame. I want to trust that the justice system pursues the guilty and protects the innocent. I want to hear an officer say, *I got*

you, and believe them. I want to be at ease during a routine traffic stop. But I can't. Because I know if I go out jogging in a hoodie at night, there's a possibility I may not come back.

To put this horror in the words of professor, thought leader, and minister Michael Eric Dyson,

> The history of race would yet again be condensed into an interaction between the cops and a young Black anybody from Black anywhere doing Black anything on any given Black night. [This] perverse predictability . . . means any Black person can be targeted anywhere at any time.
>
> I don't know how much of this resonates with you. If you look like me, you've probably got similar stories. You've probably learned how to find the humor in them as a way to process some of the trauma. But my point is not so much about law enforcement as it is about injustice and the traumatic effect it has on us—especially from places that should otherwise comfort and protect us.[1]

LET IT ALL OUT

We don't have to share an exact experience for me to know you've probably been bruised and battered, whether physically, emotionally, or spiritually.

I got you. If there's something you need to get off your chest, let it out. Imagine I'm right there with you, listening, not judging a word you say. Take your time; I'm in no rush. And when you're ready, let's give it to God.

Father,
> *I come to You broken. I've got wounds and scars no one but You can see. Heal me, Lord. Restore me. Bring people into my life who will comfort me—people I can trust, people who've got me. No matter what I've seen before, and no matter what lies ahead, I want to give it all to You.*
> > *Amen.*

Maybe you've been so beaten down, you'd rather just throw your hands up and walk away. You can't see a path forward, so you're looking for a way out. It could be a new community. It could be a new town. It could be a new church. Or maybe you aren't looking to go somewhere else. You retreat into yourself instead. Injustice has hit you so hard that you internalize it. You try to drown it in distraction. You look to keep yourself and your family safe and let the world do its own thing.

If that's where you are, I feel you. But at some point, you need to come to

No matter what, we must not lose hope.

terms with your expectations. Nothing in life is going to be everything you hoped it would be. Everything is broken, everything is tainted, even justice—especially justice. You shouldn't expect it to be otherwise, even if you've gotten it worse than other people.

You can want it to be better, yes. You can get on your knees and pray that justice is served. *Amen.* You can get up and start praying with your feet to work toward a better future. *Amen, Amen.* But what you *can't* do is lose hope.

It comes down to whether you really believe God is in control. If not, then the Teacher's got it right—the pursuit of justice really is meaningless. How so? Because even if you dismantle all the corrupt systems in the world, you'll still be left with the human heart, whose flaws created those systems in the first place. Given enough time, they'll be built right back up, even stronger than before. But if you *do* believe God is in control and take the Teacher's words to heart that God will bring all things to justice, then there is hope. And where there is hope, there is purpose.

> You can fight for justice, knowing you're doing God's work.

Because God is just, you can fight for justice, knowing that you're doing His work—however imperfectly. No matter how frustrated or tired you are, He is in your corner. Furthermore, because God's perfect justice will only come

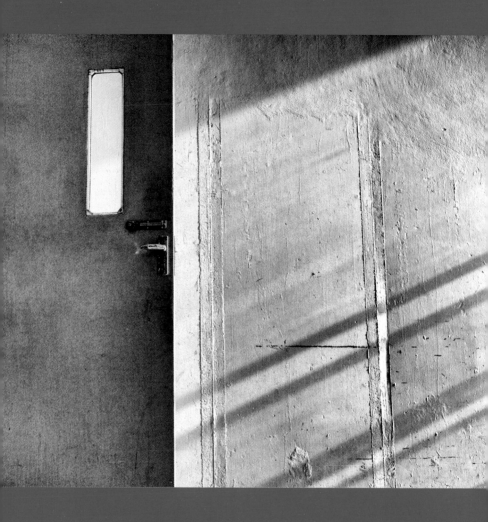

Where there is hope, there is purpose.

———————

to pass at the end of all things, you don't need to accomplish it all today. It's impossible, and you'll get discouraged if you try. This realization isn't meant to make you complacent; it's meant to fill you with courage to keep working every day.

The leaders of the civil rights movement understood. Instead of making a false choice between doing everything and doing nothing, they drew their courage and inspiration from their belief that their actions meant something in the sight of a just God. They didn't begin the journey, and they wouldn't see the end. That was in God's hands. Their task was to keep us moving further down the road in the time they were given.

Breathe

What about you? How can you help? While it's important to engage with national and global issues, especially when it comes to systemic injustice, it's also important to know there's a lot you can do at the local level. You see, once a problem is on the news, it's already reached maturity, which makes it harder to solve. So, start looking for problems in their infancy. Look to the needs of your neighborhood. Not even systemic injustice

> can stop simple acts of kindness. Get to know your neighbors. Learn their troubles. Make your house a refuge for those in need.

As I've shared over the past few chapters, you don't need big acts of service to make a big impact. Stringing a bunch of small ones together works just fine. Offer care and assurance, even if you've got nothing else to give. And through it all, *pray.*

Pray that God would look graciously on the seeds you've sown. Pray they would grow into a harvest of righteousness in your community. Pray that you would know more deeply that God's *got you,* so you can offer that assurance and peace to others, even as we live in the midst of injustice.

Injustice isn't going anywhere soon. So don't be blindsided when it hits you. Be prepared. Like the Teacher, see it for what it is—and what it isn't. Even though I'm still shaken by the injustices of my past, I haven't been blindfolded to the hope that God will deal with them in the end. And my hope in God's perfect justice keeps me going. It keeps me investing in the brokenness around me and inside me. I pray you would know that same hope. No matter where you are, or what you've known, injustice *will not win.* God's *got you.*

On that note, let me pray for you.

Father,

Thank You that You hold both of our lives in Your hands. I pray we would never lose sight of the future You promise to those who trust in You. You will judge both the righteous and the wicked. And Your judgment will be perfect. In the meantime, may that give us hope so we won't give up too soon—hope that our efforts won't be in vain. Help us anticipate what You'll finally bring to pass. Help us do our part to keep the pursuit of justice moving in the right direction. Bless us as we go.

Amen.

Frustration is better than
laughter,
because a sad face is
good for the heart.
The heart of the wise is in
the house of mourning,
but the heart of fools is in
the house of pleasure.

ECCLESIASTES 7:3-4

chapter ten

things fall apart

Jesus once told His disciples, *"In this world you will have trouble"* (John 16:33). It's gotta be one of His least popular, and most forgotten, promises. Most of us spend our lives doing all we can to steer clear of hard times. We would rather sail through life. As a matter of fact, most of the pursuits we've already explored together—knowledge, pleasure, money, and work—are attempts at hurdling over hard times, or at least making hard times more bearable. But the thing about Jesus is that He bats a thousand. He's as right about this as anything else He's said. In this world, in this life, you will have trouble. You *will* face adversity. The question is: what do you do when it comes?

Alright, this one's going to be hard—maybe harder on me than it is on you. We're not going to talk about generic adversity, like missing out on the job you were chasing or not

Ask yourself how you want to face adversity. getting a callback for a second date after you thought the first went well. This is about collapsing under the weight of a brother dying. It's dragging yourself through the valley of the shadow of death. This is about helplessly watching another brother self-destruct through self-medication—not realizing that your own self-righteousness was taking you down a different path to the same desolate destination.

Suffering is gut-wrenching. Not knowing why it's happening is crippling. It makes you feel like you'll never get back up. And while I don't have all the answers, I do have my experience—and you have yours. So, we can start this hard conversation by sharing what we've been through. I'll go first. And as I share, I am going to tell how the Teacher has helped me, if not overcome adversity, then at least find a way through it. I want to do the same for you. 'Cause when it comes to things like this, no one—not the Teacher, not me, not anyone else—can save you from heartache. It's a mountain that won't move (no matter how much faith you have). But we can tunnel through it together and seek purpose wherever it can be found.

Let's Connect

Let's begin where we're going to end: in prayer.

Father,

I know heartache is going to find its way to my doorstep, if it hasn't already. I know I'll be tempted to turn inward and turn my back on You when it comes. Maybe it's here, and I'm tempted right now. So, hear my prayer today. Comfort me. Run after me, even as I run from You. Reveal Yourself in the midst of my troubles so I might know and love You more. Give me the courage to speak honestly and listen intently.

Amen.

THE FORMULA MYTH

Throughout most of my life, adversity—and I mean the really hard kind—was only something *other* people went through. Yeah, I had that episode in Nigeria, but it was a one-off. I knew that life would have its share of bumps in the road, but at the end of the day I believed if you behaved yourself and put in the work, you'd get where you wanted to go. Basically, I thought that life had a formula. The inputs and outputs made sense. It's why I like math so much (for real—my first job out of college was as a math teacher). Math is neat, reliable, and predictable. No matter where you are or what you are doing, $2 + 2$ is always going to equal 4.

And the formula didn't just make sense for my life; it made sense of other people's lives too. Sam was a good kid who blossomed into a great man. He worked hard, made smart decisions, and followed the rules. And as far as I could tell at the time, he was going to reap the rewards of those decisions for the rest of his life.

But my older brother Emmanuel? He was Sam's opposite in many ways. He got in with the wrong crowd and into every trap laid out for a Black kid growing up in Southwest Houston. And with those bad inputs came bad outputs: addiction, jail cells, always having to look over his shoulder. It didn't give me any satisfaction to see Emmanuel like that. But it did fit my understanding of life's formula. And then Sam died young and Emmanuel kept on living. And so did I.

I've already shared about the resentment I held against Emmanuel. It wasn't fair to him. And I still don't feel I've been able to atone for it. But adversity has that effect, right? If we're not careful, it can make us lash out at the ones we love. And I love Emmanuel.

Hear me out. I'm not going to lie. I still like math, and I still like my formulas. But formulas in life are only going to get you so far. And in the wake of Sam's death, I found they didn't go nearly far enough to explain what was happening. My suffering seemed as senseless as my formulas were useless.

Breathe

If you've got people like this in your life and you're struggling to know how to feel about them, bring them to Jesus. Pray that He would help you see them with His eyes.

And if, like me, there's something you think you need to atone for, do the same: pray. Pray that He would soften your heart and give you an opportunity to make amends.

DON'T OVERDO IT

In chapter seven of Ecclesiastes, the Teacher offers a series of aphorisms—basically a tweet thread of easily digestible pieces of wisdom—easy because of their size, not their sweetness. There's a bitterness to many of his observations. Take a look:

> In this meaningless life of mine I have seen both of these:
> the righteous perishing in their righteousness,
> and the wicked living long in their wickedness.
> Do not be overrighteous,
> neither be overwise—
> why destroy yourself?
> Do not be overwicked,
> and do not be a fool—
> why die before your time?
> It is good to grasp the one
> and not let go of the other.
> Whoever fears God will avoid all extremes.
>
> **Ecclesiastes 7:15–18**

If the payout for all of Sam's hard work and good behavior was only an early grave, why bother? Why, as the Teacher says, be overrighteous? It won't save you from death. I've seen too many people torture themselves trying to be the best people they can be. They try to do everything right, never putting a foot out of place, all because they believe God will honor their many righteous sacrifices. It's a quid pro quo relationship. *God, I give You my holiness; give me Your blessing in return.*

But what kind of blessing do they expect? A prosperous life. *God just wants to bless you.* Have we so quickly forgotten that Jesus suffered and was crucified? Did we miss the part where, of the twelve disciples, only one died of natural causes?

Here's what I'm not saying. I'm not telling you to throw your morality overboard. Virtue is good. God delights in holiness. Just don't torture yourself, thinking that somehow you and God have got an arrangement. It's only going to end in bitterness and disillusionment. Like waiting in the Houston heat for a bus that's never coming, you'll just be angry at God for failing to fulfill promises He never made. Do yourself a favor; don't set yourself up for failure.

But this doesn't let the wicked off the hook either. The Teacher recognizes it's an injustice when the wicked live longer than the righteous. Yet he also observes that the wicked, in their foolishness, can just as easily die before their time. Jay-Z may have sold crack on his way to becoming a businessman, but he's the exception, not the rule. As D'Angelo says in *The Wire*, when he's explaining chess to Bodie, the pawns usually get capped quick and they're out of the game early. They almost never become queens. Jay-Z's life ain't a blueprint; it's an anomaly.

Formulas aren't going to help you overcome adversity. That's like trying to domesticate a lion. Life can't be tamed that way. So, when adversity comes, your formulas fail, and all your good habits and best intentions lead to nothing but sorrow and loss—what do you do?

What's Your Story?

Have you found that you haven't prayed to God in a while? You want to cry out to Him but you feel embarrassed? It's like asking a friend for help when you've been ignoring their calls. Lean in to God.

He's used to hearing from people when they're at their lowest points. He won't take it as a slight if this is the reason you've started praying to Him now. His door is always open, and the porch light is always on.

Don't worry about how long it's been since your last words to Him; just make sure your first ones are good and honest. Your weakness isn't a problem to Him. In fact, the biggest problem is your attempt at self-sufficiency.

While you're at it, bring your loved ones in too. Don't try to do this alone. Invite them into your prayers. Let them support you every step of the way.

INVITE HIM IN

What if you aren't facing adversity? Don't squander your prosperity. Yes, God hears you fine when things are going bad, but God hears you just as well when things are good. *Keep inviting Him in.* Get in the habit of praising God for all the good things He's doing in your life. Invite others into your thanksgiving. Set a time, at least a day each week, to pray prayers of gratitude for the good things God is bringing your way.

But whatever the case, prosperity or adversity, sunshine or rain, may your prayers only deepen your dependence upon Him.

Like I told you, these ideas aren't solutions. They aren't going to immediately lift your spirits when you are in a horrible situation. But there is meaning and purpose to be found when adversity deepens your relationships with your loved ones and your Creator. It may even lead to redemption.

And this brings me back to Emmanuel. We actually had a great relationship growing up. As a matter of fact, we used to team up against Sam! It was only when I was getting into high school that he started to dabble in drugs and we began to drift apart. At the time, I just didn't understand it. And then Sam died, and I began to see things in a new light.

Sam's death messed me up. I didn't realize how much it messed up Emmanuel. Maybe I was too caught up in my grief and bitterness. As the years passed and we fell out of touch, I had formed this idea in my mind that he was egocentric, selfishly putting everyone else through hell. He was the Prodigal Son who might never return. But there he was, back home, grieving at Sam's funeral. He *loved* his brother. He *loved* his family.

> There is meaning and purpose to be found when adversity deepens your relationships with your loved ones.

The Teacher says, *The heart of the wise is in the house of mourning* (7:4). And he's right. Nothing reveals more about life and what we really value than a funeral. Watching my oldest brother return to his family, sharing in our grief, made me realize that Sam had given us an opportunity to start again. From death came new life. It also showed me that if Emmanuel was the Prodigal Son who repented and returned home, I was the self-righteous brother who stayed behind—filled more with criticism than compassion.

As time has gone on, Emmanuel's been able to share more and more about his troubles. It turns out his life had been

From death comes new life.

———————————

rougher than he'd ever let on. He just couldn't face it. So, he ran to whatever would shut out the pain and the shame. That's where the drugs and the bad relationships came in. They were just his ways of dealing with his ever-growing burden.

And like so many of us, he's still in it. Those demons of shame, pain, and insecurity don't shake so easily. But now he's not alone. I'm just a phone call and a flight away. I'm there for him. And he knows it. (He's got his own story to tell, and he's a much better storyteller than I am. When he writes it out, I'm excited for you to read it.)

> Thank God He doesn't work according to my formula for life.

At the very depths of trouble and loss, God gave me and Emmanuel another chance. When adversity tore us down, He built us back up again. Only this time, we could do it together. And for that I thank God. Emmanuel does too. He was merciful and gracious to us both. I'm so glad God didn't work according to my formula.

SUFFERING CAN CONNECT US

I told you I wasn't going to give you any solutions, and I haven't. But I have offered you my hand. Take it if you want. Grief can feel like a mountain sometimes. It towers over you, overwhelms you. It's so high you don't even think you can climb over it. There are some without skin in the game who will tell you that the right amount of faith will throw that mountain into the sea. But faith doesn't move every mountain. Believe me, I've tried. Me and the Teacher, we're here with not much more than a hammer and chisel. But we have found a way through, even if the mountain hasn't moved.

Learn the limits of your formulas. Share your adversity with your loved ones. Lean in to God. This advice isn't going to take away your pain. It isn't going to release you from adversity. Jesus told His disciples, *"In this world you will have trouble."* But He didn't stop there. He also told them, *"Take heart! I have overcome the world"* (John 16:33). You may never understand the reasons for why you suffer. But you can use that suffering to deepen your relationship with others and, most importantly, with God. For it is His power, not yours, that has overcome the world and all its troubles.

Father,

You're wiser than me. I cannot see all that You see. I cannot know all that You know. Your grace and mercy are beyond anything I could possibly imagine. Thank You for Your patience with me. Use my adversity and prosperity to deepen my reliance upon You. Bring me closer to the ones I love. You have not made me to do this alone.

Amen.

147

Two are better than one,

because they have a good

return for their labor:

If either of them falls down,

one can help the other up.

ECCLESIASTES 4:9-10

share my world

As we've shared together, the same theme has come up time and again: *nothing in life will be everything you hoped it would be.* No matter what you're chasing, there's always something missing in the end. Perfection is just out of reach. It's like a vapor. You can see it, but you can't hold it.

You pursue knowledge, and it leads to lament. You turn to pleasure, but it doesn't satisfy. You try to get ahold of money in hopes of a better life, but it only takes hold of you. The blood, sweat, and tears of your work are just as likely to leave you with nothing but more of the same. Justice is never on time, if it ever arrives. And despite your best efforts, you can't outrun adversity any more than a dog can outrun its tail.

The Teacher's message is sobering. But now you have clarity. As you look back, you can see that only trouble is guaranteed. As you look forward, you know only to expect the unexpected. Purpose isn't in your hands, but God's. So, you trust in what you cannot see.

But we're not finished yet. We've got more to do, and we've got to do it *together*.

THE REAL RELATIONSHIP SAVER: COMMITMENT

In the last chapter we wrestled with adversity, and we saw that God can use our darkest days to restore our hope and our relationships—with Him and with each other. In this chapter we're going to devote ourselves to the *with Him and each other* part, 'cause if we're going to be surrounded by problems, we'd better be surrounded by people.

Here's what I've learned from the Teacher: *Two are better than one, because they have a good return for their labor: If either of them falls down, one can help the other up* (4:9–10). We're not meant to go it alone. And that's not just another of God's good gifts that we can take or leave. It's what He intended all along.

Relationships aren't a cure-all. They're not so much a solution to trouble as a means through it. Ask Shawndra.

I love my wife with all my heart, and she loves me with all of hers, but our love goes way deeper than romance. I've experienced the depths of my wife's love for me. Adversity sunk us to the bottom, but on that ocean floor we found something special. We surfaced with these glittering pearls of commitment.

I think a lot of folks these days believe commitment is an outgrowth of love. *I'll stay with you because I love you.* I actually think the opposite is true. Love grows out of the security and trust that comes from a real commitment to each other. It's more like, *No matter what comes your way, I'll be here, through it all.* And this isn't something exclusive to married folks. It's true of all your closest and most vital relationships. The most important thing you share is your commitment to each other. I know this because I have been sustained by its power.

> Real commitment combined with security and trust causes love to grow.

Breathe

When you have kids, you get accustomed to taking their temperature. You don't do it all the time, of course, but if they get a cough or their nose starts to run, you bring out the thermometer just to make sure something more serious isn't going on. Have you ever thought of doing something similar for your closest relationships? Maybe it's time to take their temperature.

Think about those you love most. Think about who you spend most of your time with. Take the temperatures of those relationships.

- Are they healthy?
- What's the level of commitment? Is it equally shared?

If those relationships don't have a clean bill of health, if sickness lingers, give them the care and attention they deserve. You won't regret it.

In the introduction to this book, I told you that when Sam passed I became a different person overnight. For eight years, Shawndra had been married to this one guy—an optimistic, outgoing spouse with a great sense of humor—and then, it was like everything she loved about that person died. Someone else took his place. My depression turned to self-sabotage. I tried to push everything away. Her included. When she tried to check in on me, I resented her "meddling." When she gave me space, I was bitter that she was being "distant." But Shawn stood tall. She chose to stay. She was with me, not just in the trouble that surrounded us, but in the trouble I created.

She wouldn't let it ruin me. But she also knew she needed help. When it finally got too much for her to bear alone, and I weighed her down with baggage she couldn't carry, she got reinforcements. The Teacher advises, *A cord of three strands is not quickly broken* (4:12). I've always thought he meant you need more than just two of you. The more people you've got involved who are committed to your relationship, the stronger you will be—especially in marriage.

Whenever I officiate a wedding, I always make sure to tell the congregation as we pray for the couple: *You are not spectators; you are participants.* The responsibility of the bride and groom's friends and family is not limited to showing up on the day. A time will come when the couple will need their support. They may even need to be carried. Romance is only going to get them so far. It's only going to get *you* so far. You need a team.

When Shawn walked out the door, her first thought wasn't, *Where do I go?* It was, *Who do I go to?* She went to her closest friends. When she left, my first thought wasn't, *What do I do now?* It was, *Who do I call?* If nothing else, we didn't isolate. We went to those who knew us best. And they helped bring us back from the brink.

You're a participant,
not just a spectator,
in the lives of others.

You're a p

st a

live

Come Together

You've filled out forms asking you for emergency contact information, right? It happens pretty often when you've got kids. You provide the name and number of someone who'll take care of them if something bad happens and you aren't available. But who do *you* call when life gets tough?

- Make yourself an emergency contact list.
- Write down the names of three people you can turn to in the middle of a crisis.

This way, you won't be alone, wondering, *What do I do now?* You'll know just who to call. Trust me, knowing the *who* makes the *what* less daunting. And whatever you do, don't forget to let these people know they're on your list. Offer to be on theirs while you're at it.

I didn't have to scroll through my contacts to figure out who I was going to call. It was a reflex: Richard, Moe, and Trip. In no more than five minutes, all three were at my door. Shawn was already at her friend's. This was no miracle. We all lived in the same neighborhood—not by chance, but by choice. We had committed to do life together.

When it comes to buying a house and going hundreds of thousands of dollars into debt, there are a lot of factors to consider. Will the house appreciate in value? Is it located in a good school district? Is it close to work? Your decision can say a lot about what you value. For us? It was relationships. Richard, Moe, and Trip were all pastors at our church. But more than that, they were close friends. We were committed to one another. We could share anything, and no problem was too inconvenient.

And just as importantly, we could be there for each other at the drop of a dime if needed. When people are at their lowest points, minutes matter. The difference between waiting for help for five minutes or half an hour could be the difference between a life saved or a suicide attempt. The closer you are to one another, the sooner help is on its way.

Shawndra and I have been blessed by our friends. But I know that not everyone has a shoulder to cry on. Sometimes it's hard to find someone who is as committed as you are to the friendship. Loneliness is everywhere. If you want to reach out, and aren't sure how to do it, let me give you some advice.

What's Your Story?

You've got to be okay with trailblazing. You need to be prepared to take the first step. It might be as small as asking for sugar from a neighbor or getting the name of the person serving you coffee. But you have to start the conversation.

You ain't perfect, so don't expect perfection from anyone else. They haven't been designed to meet your every emotional need. You'll crush them or alienate them if you try. So, be gracious, just as you would expect the same from them.

Invest in the people who are willing to go beyond the surface, willing to be vulnerable. This means being vulnerable too. The closest friendships are forged through adversity, when you need to lean on each other to get through. If you don't let go of your self-sufficiency, you'll never receive the benefits of real friendship.

And, of course, God cares about you having good friendships too. Ask Him for His help.

Father,
I'm looking for the kinds of friends I
can put on an emergency contact list. I

*want to be on theirs too. I'm tired of being
lonely. I'm tired of feeling misunderstood.
I don't want to waste any more energy on
relationships that don't require commitment. Help me build friendships that are
lasting—friendships that build upon You.*

Amen.

CONNECTION OVER PERFECTION

One of the biggest lessons I've learned in my life, especially
from my friends, is that the team you play with is more
important than the field you play on.

Here's what I mean. I had someone come up to me once
at church. He told me that while his business was going
great and he was making a lot of money, he felt far from
God and his relationship was struggling. *John,* he said, *I'm
drowning. I feel like I'm breaking down. How do you do it?*
By this, he meant: *You're pastoring and writing books, your
family seems well, the coffee business is thriving; yet it seems
like you've still got your life together.*

How do I do it? *I* don't *do* all these things; I'm *part* of
all these things. I always work with a team. I'm *part* of the
church. I'm *part* of Portrait Coffee. I'm *part* of my family.
I guess if I was on my own, I could have a larger piece of

the pie of some business endeavor or other creative idea, but money isn't the only thing that's valuable. In fact, some things are far more valuable. For one, there's my sanity. For another, there's my relationships.

I hate to break it to you, but I'm bad at a lot more stuff than people might think I'm good at. I don't often know what to do or what needs to be done. All I'm *really* good at is knowing who should be involved. I can put a team together and then play within it. It ain't always perfect, but it works.

When you think about attaining perfection in life, what do you think of? Does it involve compromise and consensus? Does it involve encouraging others to succeed in their strengths? Or must it involve a singular vision—*my* ideal? *I only know what it takes to make this perfect.* Here's the thing: the pursuit of perfection often leads to isolation. We think we have to do it ourselves, to make it *just right.* But that way of living is the enemy of relationships. It's the enemy of teamwork.

Because I know I'm imperfect, I'm not interested in chasing *my* ideal. If I've got an idea, I want it to be bigger than myself. That's why I want others involved. It's a perspective that helps you build teams just as it helps you build relationships. Being aware of your imperfection shouldn't lead you to despair; it should drive you toward dependence—on others and, most importantly, on God.

Perspective helps you build teams just as it helps you build relationships.

That's been God's plan all along. He's not just an add-on to a good relationship. He's the One who's going to hold it all together. Relationships are His idea, and it's been that way since the beginning.

CREATED FOR CONNECTION

Open the book of Genesis, and you'll see God look at His creation each day for six days and say, *It's good.* Do you know the first time the words *not* and *good* hold hands in Scripture? It's when Adam finds himself working alone without a hand to hold. And you know what? These words appear in the Bible *before* sin makes its grand entrance into the world. The danger of isolation predates the destruction caused by sin. God has always seen isolation as one of humanity's greatest threats to experiencing His goodness in the world.

So, God gave Adam more than a companion. He gave him a commitment—a wife named Eve! And their relationship, the very first one, can help us understand something fundamental about how to interact with others and be rooted in commitment.

But here's the thing: Jesus, not marriage, is where we see God's full answer to Genesis 2:18—*"It is not good for the man to be alone."* In Jesus, God came to live together *with us.* To show us the full extent of His love and commitment. Jesus spent His life initiating relationships with those isolated by choice or because of an illness or malady they couldn't control.

He went after the lonely, the isolated, the depressed, the hurting. He lived his life in such a way that everyone—from strangers hanging on sycamore trees to thieves hanging next to Him on crosses—understood they were created for relationship with God and one another.

Jesus knew He was going to be surrounded by problems in this life, so He surrounded Himself with people. But He also knew they couldn't—or wouldn't—support Him when times got tough. During His worst moment, as He hung on the cross, He experienced a silence from God that was soul-crushing. But those burdens didn't change an ounce of His commitment to us.

He took the punishment for our sins, experienced the lowest depth of isolation so we wouldn't have to. He took all that so He could bring us back to right relationship with God and with one another. This is a love that is *so* committed that Jesus was willing to give His life for it. This is a love that is *so* contagious that everyone who truly understands and receives it can't help but want to reproduce it.

As I said before, relationships aren't as much a solution to our troubles as a means through them. Listen: community doesn't solve all life's problems, but it does help guard us against some of their most devastating effects. We carry each other's burdens, as Jesus carries ours, all in the belief that He will redeem our suffering and wipe away our tears in the end (Revelation 21:4).

At our church, we have a saying: *We're a church where tears flow freely, but our floors stay dry.* What we mean is, having a great community around you doesn't mean you won't have problems. You will. Tears are going to fall; they just won't hit the floor. There will always be a shoulder to cry on. We grieve together, just as we rejoice together, because Jesus is committed to holding our lives together in His love.

Father,

You have created me for relationship—and for You above all. By Your Spirit, make me more like Jesus. Help me reach out to the lonely and the isolated. Help me come to You more often in prayer. When troubles come, and I'm tempted to shoulder my burdens on my own, send help! Use me in all my imperfection. Make me a committed friend—to others, and especially to You.

Amen.

163

JOHN ONWUCHEKWA

The living

know that they

will die.

ECCLESIASTES 9:5

life after death

I'm a pastor. Over the last fifteen years, I've
preached hundreds of sermons to thousands of people. I
remember three of them most vividly. They were given at
the funerals of Nailah, a sixteen-year-old girl I'd never met;
my brother Sam; and Elfreida Brown, a beloved church
mother who passed away during the early years of our community. To this day, I can still close my eyes and see those
rooms as well as faces of the people who filled them. I can
still hear their sobs. What stands out most, though, is how
unprepared most of them were to be there. Me especially.

As this book about life draws to a close, it's only appro-
priate that we should also talk about life's conclusion.
Finding purpose in all of life's joys and sorrows is only
going to get you so far before you're confronted with the

reality of the grave. I can't completely prepare you for death. But I can share with you what I've learned about living in its shadow. And I can tell you about the hope I've found in the resurrection of Jesus Christ. Death is coming, but it's not our final destination.

NONE OF US WILL ESCAPE

Take a moment to think about all the plans you have for your life. Walking across a stage with your diploma, the details of your wedding day, buying a house, getting a promotion, starting a family. You can imagine all this stuff taking place, can't you? You can see it as clearly as some of your fondest memories. But you know what? It's all just your *imagination*. There's no guarantee any of it will come to pass. That's what hallucinogens do: they make you see things that aren't really there.

Now, let me ask you another question. When's the last time you *imagined* your death? I'll let that one hang in the air for a minute. Unlike everything else you imagined so clearly, there is nothing more guaranteed than the grave—yet we find it *unimaginable*.

We usually think of death as something that happens to other people. I still remember the first time I had to break the news of someone's passing to a friend—actually, he was more like my brother. Diamone let me know Muche's brother had been murdered, and someone had to tell Muche. He was just about to speak at a college event when I came up.

What's wrong? he asked.

Muche saw something in my face and he just *knew*.

CJ's dead.

The words stumbled out of my mouth. I was ashamed

of how quickly I said it and how relieved I was to let it go. Muche went *sprinting* down the street. As if running away from me would make my words less true. I saw how bad it hurt to lose a brother. I thought I knew. But even then, his experience couldn't teach me. It couldn't completely prepare me for Sam's passing. I had to learn it for myself.

The way you see death shapes the way you live your life.

The Teacher tells us, *Death is the destiny of everyone* (7:2). We talk a lot today about finding common ground. Well, there's nothing more common to us all than the ground we'll be buried under. You could have a cigarette or a bucket of kale with every meal. You could have perfect church attendance or a membership with Bedside Baptist. It doesn't matter. Death is on its way. But I don't say this to make you sad. I want you to be sober and to see things clearly, 'cause the way you see death shapes the way you live life. I also want to prepare you.

Some people say there's no way to prepare for death. If by *prepare* they mean doing something to take away the pain and loss you feel when it happens, then they're right—there is no way to prepare. But if by *prepare* they mean develop the ability to endure the unimaginable, keep your faith in God, and desire to keep living—then of course you can. You have to. It's the only way to embrace the fullness of life with joy and with purpose.

CAN YOU . . . *PREPARE* FOR DEATH?

So, where do you go from here? Here's the first thing. *Don't forget death.* You know the stories about those folks on their deathbeds full of buyer's remorse at how they'd spent their lives? Don't end up like that. Invest your time and energy in what really matters to you, 'cause death doesn't care about your long-term plans. Take care of your people. Keep short accounts in those relationships. Don't let resentments fester. Harsh words could be chiseled in stone if a sudden loss steals the opportunity to erase them.

Remembering death is not just something you do for your own sake, though. It's also something you do for others. Y'all know how Google gives you those birthday reminders? It made me realize that we don't do the same for the anniversary of someone's death. But that's a *really* important day for those who've been left behind.

March 12. April 14. January 30. They hit me hard every single year. I'm reminded of those I've lost, and their shadow hangs over the day. Do you have your own days—and the names that go with them? If not, I'm sure you know people who do. One time I challenged our church that when someone experiences death in our community, we need to make a lifelong commitment to carry the burdens with the grieving. We remember those anniversaries together so we can

Don't forget death, but *don't fixate on it* either.

love each other more fully. An April 14 never passes when I haven't been overwhelmed by unexpected texts about my brother.

Come Together

You must have friends who have lost someone special. Maybe you know the month but don't know the specific day. Find out! Keep that day in your calendar, and make a point to call them every year and check in. It may be hard, but it can help them with the grieving process as well as remind you that death is in all our futures, so you'd better live accordingly.

Don't forget death, but *don't fixate on it* either. This might sound strange considering how difficult death is to imagine, so hear me out. Ever notice how society treats the dead and dying? They are separated from the general population—in morgues, hospitals, and care homes. But here's the thing: the lengths our society will go to hide death shows us the extent of our fixation on it. And it's a fixation that can take many forms.

Take, for instance, the pursuit of healthy eating and exercise. Now, those are *good* things to pursue. They can lead to full lives. But they can also result from an unhealthy fixation on death. Instead of producing fullness of life, they empty it of its joys. All in a desperate, and ultimately hopeless, attempt to keep death at bay.

After Sam passed, I also fixated on death, but in a different way. I found it hard to invest in relationships—even with my surviving siblings. I didn't want to lose them too. The greater the affection I had, the more I knew it was going to hurt in the end.

Death was always on my mind. After Ava came back from the hospital, I would rush over to her bed every morning just to make sure she was still breathing. Even now, my heart forgets to beat when I see a missed call from my mom. She had been the one to tell me that something was wrong with Sam. Every time I see the number, I answer, expecting the worst.

CAST OUT FEAR

Are you fixated on death? Are you so afraid of it that it's stealing your joy? If so, pray with me.

Father,

Shine Your light into the shadow death casts upon my life. Reveal the relationships I've shied away from because of the fear of loss. Show me the bad habits and patterns I've disguised as virtues. Your perfect love casts out fear, and I don't want to be afraid anymore.

Amen.

The Teacher has helped me with this *so much*. Ecclesiastes 9:1–10 lays out what I've been sharing with you: don't *forget* death; but don't *fixate on it* either. Verses 1–6 remind us not to forget the fate that unites us all. Verses 7–10 tell us to enjoy life while we have it—*Go, eat your food with gladness, and drink your wine with a joyful heart, for God has already approved what you do.* It's important to note that the Teacher's not making suggestions here. He's *commanding* you to *go. Eat. Drink. Do.* Be glad. Be thankful. Enjoy the pleasures of life *because* death is coming. Savor them before they pass. They may not make life meaningful, but that's okay. That's not their purpose. They're still good. They're a gift for the here and now.

In many ways, we talked about this in the chapter on pleasure. Remember how much Nancy enjoyed the colors in the trees? That's what I'm talking about. A sober view of death doesn't mean a diet of dust and ashes.

On the contrary, it should heighten your senses. Maybe that means embracing some things you haven't before. Try something new. Get something nice for yourself—after all, the Teacher commands you to *always be clothed in white, and always anoint your head with oil* (v. 8). You may want to give the oil a hard pass, unless you *really* want to try something new, but his point is that a greater awareness of your death should actually enliven your life, because you know it's a gift that won't last forever. So, let's enjoy it while it's here.

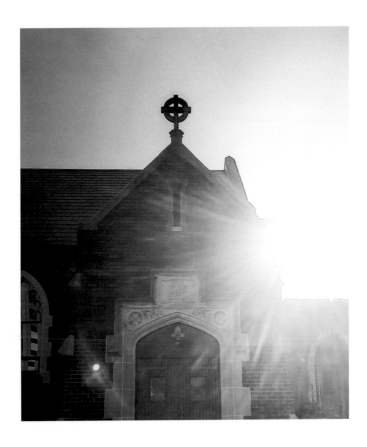

MAKE THE MOST OF IT

Read Ecclesiastes 9:7–10 and make a list of at least one way you're going to obey all of those commands.

Go: No excuses. Treat the items below as a checklist. Seize the day. Enjoy God's good gifts while you can!

Eat: Make plans to spend more money on a meal than you normally would. Savor the experience.

Drink: Get the good stuff, whatever your drink of choice is (mine's obviously coffee). Drink it slow, take your time. Have a good conversation with someone over something special.

Be clothed in white: Find some place to dress up for and go. Take your spouse, partner, friend, or go solo. Just get out!

Enjoy life: Let the person you love know how special they are today! Find something y'all enjoy doing together, and make the most of it.

Do: If you're at a crossroads in life or you're feeling stuck, choose a direction and take that first step with conviction.

Father,

Light a fire under me so I'll make the most of the time You've given me. I want to chase after life, not flee from death. Let the knowledge of my

death only make my experiences in life that much
sweeter.

Amen.

Enjoying your life is a spiritual discipline. It's being fully human—just as God created you. Joyfully receive the gifts He's given you. God's common grace for humanity involves providing pleasures to soften the blow of life's frustrations. Don't apologize for them. Don't waste them. Celebrate them.

BE PRESENT NOW

So, how do we bring it all together? How do you walk that tightrope between not forgetting about death and not fixating on it either? It seems too easy to fall off on one side or the other. This is where the Teacher's advice in Ecclesiastes comes to an end and a greater Teacher's advice begins. He shows us the way.

The Teacher in Ecclesiastes may not have believed that death was the end, but his wisdom was reserved to what he experienced *under the sun*. Jesus has shown us more. Through His death and resurrection, we have been given a taste of life—eternal life—beyond the sun. This, too, should change the way we experience life in the present.

That's what this whole book has been about. Nothing in life will be everything you hoped it would be. Nothing will change the fact that life as we know it is fundamentally broken. To spend your time trying to make heaven on earth is the equivalent of chasing after the wind—always grasping, you'll never take hold of lasting joy and true purpose. We are too broken to fix ourselves.

This is where Jesus' life, death, and resurrection are so important.

First, Jesus shows us how to enjoy the pleasures of life. The Bible says that He ate and drank and was an amazing storyteller with a good sense of humor. He was great at parties, made sure the wine didn't run out, and created deep friendships with other grown men (one miracle that's slept on more than any other). Jesus made the most of His life on earth and seemed to help others enjoy it in a rich way.

And not only that. Jesus upends everything we thought about death. He removes the finality of it. That's why the resurrection is so important. When Jesus came back to His friends and disciples, He showed them—He showed *us*— that death is not the end. It's no longer a destination, but a doorway for those who believe in Him.

This is how Jesus walked that tightrope so well. He never forgot about death, but never fixated on it either, because death was never His final destination.

Read through any of the Gospels, and you'll notice a

few things. First, Jesus constantly talked about His own death. The reasons for it and the outcomes. Our sin and salvation. He never forgot it. He was constantly reminding others that He wasn't going to be there forever. But here's the most important thing most of us miss: Jesus *never* talked about His death without talking about His resurrection. Never. They're a package deal. When He died for our sin and rose from the dead for our new lives, Jesus showed He's not one of a kind as it relates to resurrection, but the first of His kind.

But that's not all. His resurrection also reminds us that God loves His creation. Jesus returned to earth in a *body*, a body that could eat a breakfast He prepared on a beach for the ones He loved (John 21:1–14). Think about that for a second. *Eat your food with gladness. Drink your wine with a joyful heart.* That's what God would do in your place.

And finally, the resurrection shows us that our faith in Jesus is not in vain. You can trust Him with your life and know your trust is not misplaced. This means trusting Him with your death too. Life, death, and resurrection. There is nothing God can't use. None of it is meaningless in His sight. It shouldn't be in yours either.

This is the key to finding purpose in all of life's joys and sorrows, between living for something and living for nothing: we know this life isn't all there is! There's something more!

This absolutely changes the way we live our lives. Because we don't get caught up trying to make heaven on earth when we know there's something better. We're free to enjoy the pleasures and endure the sorrows in the meantime. And when we're buried underneath our common ground, we don't end there. *We go on.*

Death is a detour we all have to take to our final destination: eternity. The promise of the resurrection is available if you'll transfer your confidence from your hands to His. Now you see how we can always be aware of our death but not fixate on it either. We've been set free from the *fear* of it as a constant motivator for how we live now.

Jesus is the Way, the Truth, and the *Resurrected* Life. And that life is eternal. *Death could not hold Him in its power.* And He's made that same power available to you. Now that's worth celebrating. *Where's that wine?*

Father,

Thank You for Jesus. Thank You for His life, death, and resurrection. Help me live my life as fully as He did, enjoying the pleasures and enduring the sorrows in the sure and certain hope that death is not the end. Lord, prepare my heart. Transform my fear into greater faith. My life is in Your hands.

Amen.

where do we go from here?

Where Do We Go from Here: Chaos or Community? The title of Martin Luther King Jr.'s final book, published the year before his assassination, is the inspiration for the title of the book you now hold in your hands. Dr. King spent his life working for change. He saw the fruit of his efforts and experienced great admiration as the foremost leader of the civil rights movement.

But even where there was progress, there was also regression—and sometimes bitter opposition. He was both *Time*'s Man of the Year *and* one of the nation's most hated people. It is fitting then that his last work didn't give a definitive answer. It offered a question: *Where do we go from here?*

JOHN ONWUCHEKWA

Dr. King's life had a purpose. He had hoped to arrive at a destination. But on the day before he died, during his famous speech "I've Been to the Mountaintop," he acknowledged that though he'd seen the Promised Land, he might never get there. And he was right. Did this make his life meaningless? Of course not. Even as he seemed to anticipate his assassination, he was serving happily.

Weighed down by trouble, but his spirit filled with enough hope to make sure no one around him was drowning in despair. The state of his soul wasn't affected by the state of his surroundings. He wasn't worried about anything. Why? Because, *Mine eyes have seen the glory of the coming of the Lord.*

This book is both something of an answer to Dr. King's question and an affirmation of his life and hope in the world to come. It's about where we go from here, finding purpose in all of life's sorrows and joys. And so we've learned from the Teacher's experience in Ecclesiastes. We've wrestled with the apparent meaninglessness of life. We've embraced the seasons in our lives as we circle a greater center. We've remembered our Creator, and we've learned to *let Him cook*! And we took those lessons, shared our experiences, and explored some of life's foremost pursuits.

We saw how knowledge leads to lament, pleasure to dissatisfaction, money to slavery, work to worry, and justice to hopelessness. But we also found purpose in knowing

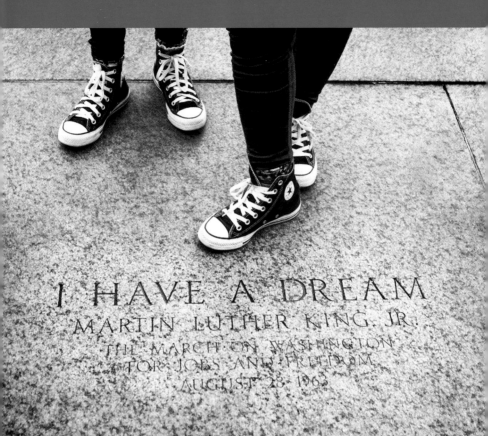

Where do we go from here? *We go on.*
Together and with purpose.

———————

God, enjoying His gifts, giving our money, finding satisfaction in our work, and trusting in the promise of God's righteous judgment. Adversity is coming, but it can bring us closer to God and those we love. Troubles will surround you, so surround yourself with people.

Be committed to living together according to God's design. Death is certain, but it's not the end. The life, death, and resurrection of Jesus Christ only makes your life more valuable, only gives you more reason to enjoy the time you've been given.

So, where do we go from here? *We go on.* Together and with purpose.

Let's pray.

Father,

Thank You for this time together. Thank You for all we've shared. It's been a hard journey, but a good one. Help us see clearly as we go on. Help us live with purpose. Fill us with Your love and wisdom. Draw us closer to Yourself and to each other. May we live full lives in this fractured world as we await the hope of the Resurrection.

In the name of Jesus,

Amen.

reflections

I'm a quitter. I don't say it as an indictment: it's really more of an indicative. Quitting comes easier for me than I'd care to admit. I love starting things; it's the finishing that's difficult. Over the years I've learned if I'm ever going to finish something, then I can't be the only one involved. *I* don't finish much. *We* do. There are more people to thank than words will allow, so I'll highlight a few.

To my wife, Shawndra. I'm glad you're not the type to rub "I told you so" in my face. I think you don't say it often because you love to hear me say it. Well, let me satisfy you. You told me so. You've pushed me to do things that I never thought I could start, or finish. When I was ready to throw this in the trash, you rearranged our lives to provide the space for me to give time to it. You wouldn't let me quit. You

185

never do. I'm better because of you. This book is a tangible expression of your determination, not mine.

To Danielle Peterson. My acquisitions editor and my friend. I thought this message was too beautiful to be relegated to the drab living quarters that is a book with a nice cover and black and white words in between. You convinced me that we could put words on the cover and fill the book with pictures. You are as much a part of this project as anyone else. You saw every iteration of this—from idea, to almost completed, to rewritten, to now. Thanks for approaching me all those years ago, hearing me talk about my first book, asking if I wanted to write another one. Thanks for initiating the conversation and treating this project as if it was your own. The countless convos and encouragements are the only reason we're here today.

To Jennifer Moorman. You're the best! I'm excited for your next season of work. You take everything you touch and make it better. When anyone smiles reading the words, I want them to know you're responsible. I gave you a block of stone; you sculpted something beautiful.

To Steve Watts. My man. You came through at the eleventh hour and helped finish it. We limped across the finish line together. Thanks for stepping out of the whirlwind of your life to help me pick up the pieces. Can't wait to cook up more stuff with you!

To Cornerstone Church. Thanks for letting me be your pastor and discover so many of these truths with you.

To Keith Pinckney. You came by the crib almost every morning while I was working on this. You could see the tension on my forehead. Your passing statements of encouragement left a lasting impression on me. I was calmer after you left each day and able to put some words on the page. Appreciate you, my dude!

To Sam. I love you, and I hope you're proud of the man I'm becoming. You continue to shape me in ways you never expected or intended. This one's for you, bro, and for your beautiful kids. Thanks for preparing me to live in this world without you. I never imagined I'd have to start that journey as soon as I did. I kind of feel like the Karate Kid. You set me up to do things I never imagined. Love you.

reflections

Chapter 6

1. Chapter 6

   The quote from C. S. Lewis on page 82 was
   excerpted from his book *Mere Christianity*, published by
   HarperCollins, p. 58, Kindle edition.

Chapter 9

1. Chapter 9

   The quote from Michael Eric Dyson on page 127 was
   excerpted from his book *Long Time Coming: Reckoning
   with Race in America*, published by St. Martin's Press, p. 2.